6,000,000 MINUTES ON THE CLOCK

WORKING FOR MEANS AND MEANING

Mark DiGiovanni

Copyright 2008, 2015 Mark DiGiovanni
All Rights Reserved

6,000,000 MINUTES ON THE CLOCK

To Beth

For Mara

TABLE OF CONTENTS

FIRST OF ALL – WHY?
Why Do You Need This?
Why Does An Organization Exist? ~ Whysdom

HOW DID WE GET HERE?
Better Things to Do ~ They Wanted It More
Hit Any Key to Continue ~ It Worked for Darwin
What Have You Got for Me? ~ Love It or Leave It
Free Agents All ~ Flood Brings Sea Change
Destigmatized ~ Freedom Isn't Free

WHO DO YOU THINK YOU ARE?
The Sweet 16 ~ A Little Temperamental ~ The Big Five
The Big M.O. ~ You're Such a Character!
To Thine Own Self Be True

WHAT DRIVES YOU?
Flipping Pyramids ~ Motivation is Good;
Inspiration is Better ~ Master of Your Domain
Getting Along ~ Goal(s)! ~ 80/20
Good Enough is Often Better

WHAT ARE YOU THINKING?
Risk and Reward ~ The Devil You Know
Trade-Ups and Trade-Offs ~ Going Solo
Low, Medium, or High Risk? ~ It's Not What They Do;
It's Who They Are ~ A Calculated Leap of Faith
Burning Bridges

6,000,000 MINUTES ON THE CLOCK

WHERE DO YOU THINK YOU'RE GOING?
Catch the Right Bus ~ Revolving Doors
Are You Worth It? ~ Money and More
How They Rank & How They Rank 'Em

WHAT ARE THEY SAYING ABOUT YOU?
Your Life On a Page ~ Sartorial Perfection ~ The Unsaid
The Said ~ A Class Act ~ Face Time
What's Out There On You?
Fingernails on a Blackboard
Condemned By Your Own Hard Drive
Resume' or Eulogy?
If You Don't Remember Anything Else…

WORKING WORDS OF WISDOM

REFERENCES

FIRST OF ALL - WHY?

Why Do You Need This?

Let's do the math first. In America, according to a Gallup poll in 2014, the average work day is 9 hours and 20 minutes, or 560 minutes. According to the U.S. Census Bureau, the average round-trip commute to work is 51 minutes. The average American works 240 days a year. So far, that's (560 + 51) x 240 = 146,640 minutes per year devoted to work.

Most people get on the clock right after high school. It doesn't matter whether you get a job or go to college; it's still work. College merely delays the financial benefit of the work. So, you begin this odyssey around age 18. How long you have to work is a function of several variables, which include your ability to save money and live below your means, your preference between security and opportunity, and your life expectancy and lifestyle after retirement. Since the life expectancy of an 18 year-old today is about 75 *additional* years, and since even good savers can expect to work 2 years to afford 1 year in retirement, it is reasonable to expect to spend *50 years* in the workforce. Multiply the 146,640 minutes per year by 50 years and you get 7,332,000 minutes. Even if your workday, including commute, were only 8 hours per day, at the end of 50 years you would have racked up 5,760,000 minutes. Close enough.

The staggering amount of time Americans spend at work (we lead all developed nations in this category) is reason enough to read this book. Even a minor improvement on such a large investment can pay huge dividends, emotionally and financially.

A great deal of our self-worth is connected to the work we do. We aspire to jobs that not only pay well, but that also earn the admiration (even envy) of others and that might even make us famous.

When you meet someone for the first time, one of the very first questions you're asked is what you do for a living. Even the phrasing of the question is interesting. They don't ask what you do to earn money; they ask what you do for a living. You are what you do, or so it is assumed. You may place other roles such as spouse, parent, or American above your role at work, but that last role is the one that most identifies you in the eyes of others.

When something contributes so much to your identity and self-concept, it is very important that you find a good fit for who you are and who you want to be. Your job can pay psychological as well as financial benefits. Your job can also exact a huge psychological toll if it's the wrong job for you. At the very least, you don't want to spend half a century, when asked what you do for a living, responding with something like "I'm a claims adjuster (but I really wanted to be an astrophysicist)."

Half of the money earned in most private sector fields is earned by the top 10% in that field. This is something financial advisors, realtors, and brain surgeons have in common with NFL quarterbacks. In terms of earnings, the top 10% in many fields earn as much as the remaining 90%. The free market pays for performance, and the free market says that the top 10% accomplish as much as the other 90%.

6,000,000 MINUTES ON THE CLOCK

That's the private sector. Jobs in the public sector and jobs where compensation is determined separately from one's productivity (such as union jobs) do not have as strong a correlation between pay and performance. As a result, those with the most talent and ambition have historically gravitated to the private sector. Such people do not worry about having a floor of income; they just don't want a ceiling on their income.

Money is how the world tells you how much they value the work you do. When one job pays more than another, the implication is that the higher paying job is more valued by the world; therefore, the person who performs it is more valued. Being paid more is rewarding in that you have greater buying power. More pay gives our egos a boost, and it increases our status in the eyes of others.

The discrepancies in incomes in various occupations can often seem ridiculous. On its face, it is hard to defend a quarterback making $10,000,000 a year, while a special education teacher makes $40,000. The teacher's work is critical; the quarterback merely provides entertainment. The reason the quarterback makes so much more is that, while he provides a discretionary service in the form of entertainment, he provides it to millions of fans. The teacher provides a critical service, but only to a very few. **If making large sums of money is your goal, it is better to make a few dollars from the masses than to try to get large sums from a few.**

No matter how much you love your work, you would be unlikely to continue doing it if you weren't paid. More money is the major motivator in most job changes. It may be difficult to compare job-related factors like satisfaction or stress, but you always know which job pays more.

For better or worse, most of our contact points with the outside world are through money. Our work and the pay we receive for doing it are just the most obvious example. Because money is easy to measure, people often assume that a move to a higher-paying job is always the right thing to do. Everything else being the same, that logic would be correct. However, there are many other factors to consider that have nothing to do with money. When people choose or change jobs or careers based on the pay alone, they are very likely to regret the change down the road.

The right career is one where you go to work every day and think, "I would want to do this work *even if* they didn't pay me." The wrong career is one where you go to work every day and think, "I don't want to do this work *despite* the fact that they pay me."

To sum it up, here's why you need this book:
- You're likely to spend more hours at work than at any other waking activity in your life. It's a big investment.
- Your work will define you to the outside world more than anything else you do. It may also be the main way you define yourself. For better or worse, you are what you do.
- Money is the most indispensable tool in co-existing with the outside world, and for almost all of us, our only source of money is our work. You want to get the maximum return on your investment.

6,000,000 MINUTES ON THE CLOCK

Why Does an Organization Exist?

The mission statement of any organization should state clearly and succinctly why that organization exists. An organization that doesn't have a mission statement may not know why it exists. An organization that has the kind of mission statement includes nonsense like "increase shareholder value" doesn't know why they exist, either.

The goal of an organization should not be to do business with anyone who simply wants what you have. It should be to focus on the people who believe what you believe. When we are selective about doing business only with those people who believe in our WHY, trust emerges. My clients tell me that trust is the single most important factor in our relationship. They can't trust me unless they have a clear understanding of why I do what I do. They don't buy what I do – they buy why I do it.

In your relationship with any employer, you should clearly understand:
- **Why that organization exists**
- **Why they want you to be part of that organization**
- **Why you want to be part of that organization**
- **How you can help the organization fulfill its mission**

Whysdom for You

Think back to your own experiences as a student. The most boring and uninspiring classes you took were probably ones that only asked "who?", "what?", "when?", and "where?" questions. You memorized data, regurgitated it back to the teacher, and were rewarded or punished based on your ability to perform that task.

Even if you were good at that task, you probably received little intrinsic reward for what you had memorized.

The most inspiring, mind-altering classes you took probably asked a very different question - "why?" The difference between the first group of questions and the second is the difference between the left and right brain. The left brain is the analytical, computer-like part of the brain. The right brain is where our curiosity, our creativity, even our humanity reside. Asking "why?" engages the right brain. Asking "why?" lights a fire. Those other questions are merely filling buckets.

When you understand why you need to know something, the who-what-when-where questions become interesting to answer, which means the answers also become easier to retain. If students in a history class can learn why a war was fought several centuries ago, they are much more likely to remember who the combatants were, where the war was fought, and when it took place. And if they don't first learn why a war was fought, what's the point of even learning the other facts?

Don't just seek wisdom; **seek WHYSDOM – becoming wise by asking why.** Millennials are naturally good at this. Knowing why you are doing something is essential if you are to keep doing it when obstacles get in the way. A good boss should be able to tell you why your job is important or why a particular task needs to be performed in a particular manner. A good boss is not one who responds to a why question with "Because I said so!" As long as you are not acting like an over-inquisitive child, you should not be treated like one.

6,000,000 MINUTES ON THE CLOCK

HOW DID WE GET HERE?

Imagine living in a society where two-thirds of the adult population must work full-time in an effort to keep a killer under control. Because of the tremendous manpower (and womanpower) needed to fight this killer, progress in a multitude of areas, from science to civics, is stymied. Yet, despite the back-breaking efforts of millions, this killer succeeds hundreds, even thousands of times each year.

Better Things to Do

In 1840, when steam engines, trains, and the whole Industrial Revolution were heating up, 70% of the American workforce was engaged in agriculture to feed our population of 17,000,000. There were over 6,000,000 farmers. Even at that ratio, malnutrition was common, and starvation was not unknown. Even when adequate food supplies could be raised, preserving and transporting it to the people in cities were logistical nightmares.

Today, barely 2% of the workforce is in agriculture, which comes to about 2,000,000 farmers. Yet, they feed our nation's population of over 300,000,000, with plenty left over to export to other countries.

Food production has become so efficient that a single farmer today produces enough food for 150 people, compared to just 3 people in 1840. The cost of food, as a percentage of income, is the lowest in the history of the world. As a result, much of the world has stopped worrying about starvation and started worrying about obesity. Some may say we've gone from being killed from too little food to killing ourselves from too much food.

Agriculture is an example of the one constant in the ever-changing world of work - tasks continue to be done more and more efficiently. This constancy is to be expected. **In the ever-changing world of work, two aspects never change - knowledge is cumulative, and competition is relentless.** If we don't use what we already know to learn more and to become more productive and efficient, we will lose out to our competitors.

Many people look at the changes in agriculture and see only the loss of jobs and the breakup of the family farm. While such change may be sad, if agriculture were as efficient today as it was in 1840, we would need 100,000,000 more farmers than we have. Those 100,000,000 would not be available to work in other areas like:
- Finding a cure for AIDS
- Developing a pollution-free automobile
- Building a new hospital
- Taking care of elderly in a nursing home
- Creating software
- Writing books
- Teaching preschoolers

…and thousands of other jobs, all of which improve our quality of life and also create new and better jobs for a growing population. Also, if all those jobs in agriculture still existed, food would be so expensive, few of life's luxuries would be affordable, and many of what we consider to be necessities would be unaffordable, too.

6,000,000 MINUTES ON THE CLOCK

They Wanted It More

General Motors in the 1950's was almost broken up by the federal government because they had over two-thirds of the U.S. auto market; they were being called a monopoly. Today their market share is closer to 20%, and they are a little more than a shell of their former self.

Until the 1970's, the Japanese automakers' share of the U.S. market was very small, less than 5%. The American automakers did not see them as a threat. The Japanese made small cars that were not as profitable as the big cars Americans had been buying for years.

Then in 1973 came the Yom Kippur war between Israel and its Arab neighbors. Gas prices doubled almost overnight, and there were shortages and long lines at the gas pumps. People started looking for alternatives to the gas hogs they currently owned.

Nineteen-seventy-three was also the first year for a new car, the Honda Civic. What Americans discovered when they test drove a Honda or Nissan or Toyota was that, in addition to being fuel-efficient, these cars were well-made and vastly superior to their American competitors, like the Ford Pinto, Chevrolet Vega, and AMC Gremlin. A trend toward foreign cars began that continues to this day.

Back then, the American automakers had a virtual monopoly on the American market. Their only competition was among themselves, and none of them were going to make a great effort to increase market share as long as profits for all of them were good.

The Japanese automakers forced a change in the auto business. They were hungry for a share of the U.S. market, and they were willing to offer a better car at a lower price to get it. To succeed, the Japanese carmakers had to get their employees to think harder and to work harder.

For the U.S. automakers, it was time to discard old habits. Complacency was dead. Competition now came from all over the world. Workers and management now had to cooperate with each other, not confront each other. They had to start making better cars, more fuel-efficient cars, and they had to produce these more efficient cars more efficiently. Everyone's job was on the line. It was hang together, or hang separately.

"We found someone overseas who can drink coffee and talk about sports all day for a fraction of what we're paying you."

Job security became less a function of how big your employer was and more a function of how well you did your job. Costs were constantly being cut to remain competitive. Greater productivity from everyone was required. The unproductive employee (deadwood) was no longer tolerated. As would happen with almost every other sector of American business, employment with a large corporation no longer meant lifetime job security.

6,000,000 MINUTES ON THE CLOCK

To fully understand the potential consequences of underestimating a competitor and believing that the status quo is good enough, one need only look at the once-great city of Detroit today.

Hit Any Key to Continue

The typical desktop computer of today has more computing power than existed in the entire world in 1950.

In 1971, I took a graphic arts class. One of the first required projects required using a platen printing press. This process involves arranging individual metal letters and spaces backwards to print something. The process was slow and painstaking, and the quality of the product was inconsistent. The platen printing process was still in use in 1971, essentially unchanged from the time Johannes Gutenberg invented it around over 500 years earlier.

Barely four decades later, this book is being written on a PC. I can choose between hundreds of fonts and sizes; spacing is automatic; I can add graphics, and I can print everything out in full color. Within a week of completing the final proof-reading, hard copies and electronic versions of the finished product will be available online to almost everyone around the world.

The equipment that enables me to accomplish this feat costs about 9 days' wages for the average worker. The book retails for about 2 hours' wages for the lowest-paid worker in the nation. When they were published in 1455, Gutenberg's Bibles sold for the equivalent of 3 years' wages for the average worker. They were still only a fraction of the cost of the hand-printed Bibles that preceded them, which could take 20 years to complete.

6,000,000 MINUTES ON THE CLOCK

The technology on your lap or in your pocket is amazing, especially compared to what existed barely two decades ago. It's exciting to think how much more this technology will advance in the next twenty years. It's also a little scary.

The learning never ends. There will always be new discoveries, new inventions, and new technologies. If you are going to be gainfully employed in the future, you will have to learn about these new creations, and learn how to use them to be better at what you do for a living. For those of you unwilling to even learn how to program your DVR, here is your wake-up call.

Anyone who thinks education ends with a diploma or a degree is grossly misinformed. **A college degree tells a potential employer that you are trainable on a higher level.** You should not assume that your degree has taught you all you need to know to perform a job properly. Your new employer certainly understands this. They will prove it to you starting on day one of your employment. Once you earn your degree and enter the workforce, your *real* education can now begin.

It Worked for Darwin

Every job is in one of four phases:
1. Creation
2. Evolution
3. Reduction
4. Extinction

Let's start with jobs that already exist.

Most jobs will continue but will be constantly evolving. People won't gravitate to jobs that are being reduced or are becoming extinct. They will seek the ones that seem to have a future. Competition will be strong for the better positions. **One of your greatest assets in an evolving job will be your ability to learn and adapt quickly.**

There are likely to be two divergent trends in job evolution. The first will involve the breaking up of jobs into smaller and smaller tasks. The tasks will be assigned to the lowest cost producer. In the future, a job of today could have part of it done by a computer and part of it done by an Indonesian. The tasks that will stay are the ones that are done most efficiently by the person currently doing it. All tasks will be constantly reviewed to see if they are being done as efficiently as possible.

At the same time, many new jobs will be created that coordinate many tasks. The people doing these jobs won't *perform* many tasks; their job will be to *coordinate* many tasks.

For example, in the past, people have used a stockbroker, an insurance agent, an accountant, an attorney and others to plan and protect their financial future. There was rarely any coordination among these people. They often worked at cross purposes, to the detriment of the client. The Certified Financial Planner developed to fill a need to oversee and coordinate these functions.

The more complicated systems become, individuals who see the bigger picture and bring the pieces together to run more smoothly will be in demand. They will have the jobs of power, prestige, and pay in the future.

Many jobs will continue, but with a reduced number of workers doing them. An example would be TV repair. As long as we have TVs, there will always be some need for people to fix them. More often, people will replace, rather than repair a TV.

6,000,000 MINUTES ON THE CLOCK

A job being reduced still evolves for the people still doing it. TVs continue to evolve; so will the job of the TV repair people, even while there are fewer of them. Jobs in this category can be doubly stressful – you have the pressure of upgrading your skills and becoming more efficient, while at the same time wondering if you will survive the next big shakeout.

Jobs will become extinct for one of two reasons:
- There's no market for the goods or services produced, or
- A machine is more efficient at producing it.

Some jobs get totally eliminated by newer technologies. Eastman Kodak, which once employed nearly 150,000, now employs less than 20,000. The development of digital imaging virtually killed the film business, Kodak's bread and butter for over a century. In 1979, General Motors employed 680,000 people in North America. They produced 6.4 million vehicles, an average of 9.4 per employee. In 2009, General Motors filed for bankruptcy protection. During that year, their 112,000 North American employees produced 3.3 million vehicles, an average of 29.5 per employee. Kodak's workforce shrunk by 85% because there was no longer a market for their biggest product, film. GM's workforce shrunk by a similar percentage, partly because sales declined by nearly half. However, over 250,000 GM jobs vanished because robots and computers enabled vehicles to be built by fewer people. Over the last three decades, machines have replaced a quarter-million humans at GM's North American plants alone.

The following is a direct copy from a web site home page, www.thefutureofwork.net :

Future of Work is an active global community of

organizations and individuals who believe in the power and importance of collective intelligence in creating the future. Our focus is on the changing nature of work, the workforce, the workplace, and management practice. We help organizations **reduce their cost of operations and workforce support by 30% or more** while creating work environments that attract and retain the best and brightest talent - by providing strategic guidance, change readiness assessments, executive learning, and program management. (The emphasis in the above paragraph is theirs, not mine.)

To know what jobs will exist in the future requires imaginative thinking. As you look at any current job and wonder what future there is in it, ask yourself:
- How can this job be done more efficiently?
- Can someone in another country do this job as well and cheaper than it is currently being done?
- Can technology, especially new technology, come along and change or eliminate this job?
- Is the type of business the job is part of growing, changing, or dying?

What requires more imagination is to look at where we are now and figure out how a situation can be made better. A basic axiom of economics is "Find a need and fill it." With so many of our needs already filled, that axiom could be expanded to include "Find a want and fill it." Wants fulfilled have a habit of becoming needs, which improves job security. Columnist George Will says that Americans define a need as a 48-hour old want, so there is security in finding wants and filling them.

Basic necessities like food, clothing, and shelter are not likely to provide many new jobs, even if the population increases. Those jobs will become more efficient at the same time. New jobs in older industries are likely to center on improving efficiencies. Those jobs will focus on reducing the number of workers in that industry.

Fortunately for job growth, new inventions become new necessities. Examples include automobiles, television, the internet, microwaves, and cell phones. Five generations ago, the automobile didn't exist. Three generations ago, television didn't exist. Microwaves, cell phones, and the internet are all less than forty years old. They are as necessary to our daily routine as the automobile, the electric light, or the toilet.

What Have You Got for Me?

What you can offer the world comes down to three categories: your physical skills, your left-brain skills, and your right-brain skills.

Your physical skills may be highly developed, or very basic. Some examples of high-skills jobs would be those of a professional athlete or musician. If you are born with a certain physical ability and if you develop it and it is marketable, you can make a living. The professional athlete or musician is well paid because of a rare, highly developed skill that can be mass-marketed to a large audience. The ability to make money with a highly developed skill is one of the main reasons people will spend years developing that skill, with no guarantee of a financial payoff for the sacrifice. The potential payoff is one reason you see so many young men working for a chance to play in the NFL. The lack of a potential payoff is one reason you see so few young men working to become a great mime.

Basic Physical Skills (BPS) jobs may be along the lines of framing a house or cooking a meal. The level of

6,000,000 MINUTES ON THE CLOCK

pay depends on:
- the number of people who can and will do the same work (the competition)
- the number of people who will pay for the service
- the amount they are willing to pay (the market).

Since BPS jobs can be done by a large number of people, the pay scale never gets too high. The skills required to do the job are basic, so there are few barriers to entry. As the pay rises for a particular job, more people start to do it. Many of these jobs get filled by new immigrants to the U.S. and increasingly by people in other countries, if the job can be moved overseas. People gravitate to the highest paying job for which they are qualified. The job gravitates to whoever can adequately do the job for the lowest wage. These two factors, taken together, keep any basic skills job from becoming a high-paying job.

In addition to competition from other people, someone in a BPS job faces competition from machines. The Japanese automakers got a jump on their American counterparts in the 1970's and 80's by automating much of the assembly process. The robots replaced human labor and were more reliable and less expensive. The quarter-million jobs that General Motors shed over the last thirty years were due to the ability of machines to perform the same tasks as the workers; only to do it better, faster, and cheaper.

Some jobs aren't eliminated, but are changed by automation. The job of the house framer (the one who puts up the 2 by 4 and plywood framing of a house) was transformed by the invention of the air-powered nail gun. Not only could one person now do the work faster and better, he no longer needed as much strength to do it. Fewer framers were needed, and the pool of potential framers was increased because the physical requirements were relaxed.

Your left brain is the logical, analytical part. It consumes and analyzes data, much like a computer. Unfortunately, as computers improve, more and more of our left brain functions can be done by computers. It's almost impossible now for even the best chess players to beat a computer at chess. Supercomputers can analyze 200,000,000 positions per second. Even a chess app for a mobile phone can analyze 20,000 positions per second. How can a human brain compete with that?

Jobs utilizing left brain skills generally have better working conditions and pay more than BPS jobs. They are also at risk of being eliminated. These are usually good paying jobs. There is incentive for employers to eliminate unnecessary workers to reduce costs.

For example, eliminating a framer's job paying $10 per hour saves an employer $20,000 a year in wages. If more is spent in a year on a substitute, money is lost. The employer is better off keeping the framer at $10 per hour.

A different employer has a data analyst on the payroll at $50,000 a year. That employer could spend up to $50,000 a year to replace the data analyst through automation and come out ahead. The automated replacement can also work 24/7/365, doesn't need health insurance, and won't gossip about the boss behind his/her back. The higher the salary, the more motivated the employer is to find a substitute. High union wages at General Motors were a great incentive to replace workers with robots whenever possible.

In addition to automation, left brain jobs are vulnerable to outsourcing. Left brain jobs involve data.

6,000,000 MINUTES ON THE CLOCK

Data can be transported instantly from anywhere to anywhere. There aren't physical limitations to where the work can be done. If a data analyst in India can do the job of a data analyst in Indiana for half the wage, that job is likely to end up in India.

Left brain skills are a prerequisite for most future jobs. You will have to prove you can perform certain functions just to gain entry to most jobs. You will most frequently demonstrate this ability with a piece of paper - a college degree being the most common requirement.

It is important to understand what the college degree tells a potential employer. With few exceptions, it does not tell any potential employer that you have the training to tackle that new job right away. **Your college degree tells a potential employer that:**

- **You are willing to delay gratification for a more worthwhile long-term goal.**
- **You are willing to jump through many hoops on command to reach your goals.**
- **You have the basic intelligence and skills to be trained at the higher level the employer needs you to reach to become a true asset to the organization.**

Your left brain probably did most of the work that got you the job. Once ensconced in that job however, you better get your right brain working if you want to keep it.

The right brain performs all the functions that make humans unique and irreplaceable. It is the emotional side – love, hope, faith, and fear all dwell there. From the right side come perception, intuition, creativity, concepts, hunches, fantasies, humor, curiosity, analogies, and relationships. **The jobs that can't be eliminated are the jobs that utilize the unique talents of the right brain.** The jobs that utilize the right brain can't be eliminated because, at this time, there is nothing on earth that can replicate what the right brain of a human being does.

The irreplaceable jobs not only utilize the right brain, they are also a product of the right brain. Utilizing your right brain in your current job makes you that much more likely to create your own next job. It takes someone with imagination (a product of the right brain) to think outside the box and come up with a new way to use one's skills. Your dream job may exist right now, but in no place but your right brain. It's up to you to extract it.

Love It or Leave It

The single most important feature of your next (and every future) job is that you love it. Nothing stimulates the right brain like doing something you love to do, something for which you have a passion. There is a direct correlation between doing what you love and gaining economic advantage. It's hard to be good at something to which you're indifferent. In addition, if you're not good at your job, it won't be your job for long. As Albert Schweitzer, winner of the Nobel Prize said, "Success does not lead to happiness; happiness leads to success." If you find something you love to do, you will be happy. If you are happy, you are much more likely to be successful in that work.

Some younger people may be feeling pressured by others (parents, advisors, other well-meaning adults) to go into a particular career field. Their reasons might include some of the following:
- It's a growing field in the future.
- There's job security.

6,000,000 MINUTES ON THE CLOCK

- You can make a nice living.
- It's a prestigious career.
- It's a lot better than what *you're* thinking of doing!

All of these claims may be valid. They can be plusses in choosing a career, but they ignore the most important ingredients – a talent and a passion for your chosen line of work. Later, we'll look at determining your areas of talent. Let's talk about your passions now.

Passion is a right brain function. Your love of what you do is right brain – the talent to perform it is left brain and/or physical in origin. It's thought-provoking that you can find accountants and lawyers writing novels and painting pictures in their spare time, but you rarely find an artist working on a tax return or brushing up on the penal code for fun. No six-year-old boy in the history of the planet, when asked what he wanted to be when he grew up, replied "Insurance Underwriter".

Passion means you love doing your job so much that the pay you get is like icing on the cake. Your passion is your cause – the money is just the effect. Mondays don't scare you; you might actually look forward to them.

Passion means you willingly put up with all the downsides to a particular job in order to work in that field. A passionate veterinarian accepts that getting bitten, scratched, kicked, and urinated on by patients comes with the turf.

Find what you are passionate about and make it your life's work. There is no more important prerequisite to success. Speaking on behalf of the world, we don't need any more ambivalent attorneys who are only doing it to make their mothers happy.

6,000,000 MINUTES ON THE CLOCK

Free Agents All

This section is dedicated to Curt Flood. He's the reason you can't invest too much emotionally in your favorite sports team any more. He's the reason you can't invest too much emotionally (or anything else) in your employer any more. Maybe that's dumping too much on Curt. Some background is in order here.

Curtis Charles Flood was a baseball player – a good one. He was a three-time All-Star and won the Gold Glove seven straight times (1963-69). He hit over .300 six times in his fifteen-year major league career. From 1964 through 1968, his St. Louis Cardinals won two World Series championships in three appearances.

At the end of the 1969 season, the Cardinals attempted to trade Flood to the Philadelphia Phillies. At that time, baseball had the Reserve Clause. It bound a player in perpetuity to the club who owned his contract.

Flood objected to the restrictions on offering his services to others. He challenged the legality of the Reserve Clause. The case made it to the U.S. Supreme Court, which ruled against Flood in 1972. Though he lost the case, Curt Flood's lawsuit was a catalyst for change. By 1975, free agency was becoming the standard in baseball, and eventually in other sports.

Flood Brings Sea Change

Curt Flood's pioneering of free agency in

professional sports carried over into the corporate world in the coming years. There was one major difference, though. In professional sports, the free agency was initiated by the employees. A competitive bidding process for their services would increase their salaries. In 1975, the average major league baseball salary was $45,000. In 2015, the average salary was over $4,000,000. It worked.

In the corporate world, free agency was initiated by employers as a way to reduce staff and payrolls. After employers started moving away from the concept of lifelong employment, employees started to test the waters to see what they were worth on the open market.

The changes initiated by Curt Flood reverberate in the workplace today. Even employment in a stable Fortune 500 company is no guarantee of a job for life. While such changes may create more stress for the average employee, it has also created opportunity. With the mindset of a free agent and with tools like the internet, anyone can regularly check out other opportunities in the job market. You no longer just assume there is or isn't something better out there. You have the ability to know for sure. If there is something better, you can go after it. If there isn't, you stay put, content in the knowledge that you are in the best place to be for the present.

In many countries in Europe, labor contracts and other regulations limit an employer's ability to discharge unneeded workers. By handcuffing an employer's ability to fire, it also has the effect of handcuffing their ability to hire. Employers don't want to hire someone if they can't fire them if the situation requires it. They make do with whoever is already on the payroll. Unfortunately, productivity suffers, and they lose the ability to compete. With companies not hiring, employees are unable to take advantage of one of the great benefits of free agency - rising wages as a result of open bidding for them. Such restrictions help explain why unemployment rates in many countries in Europe run two to three times the unemployment rate in the U.S.

In the U.S., the increased ability and willingness of employers and employees to seek their most efficient use is one reason the U.S. economy has remained strong. Even during down cycles, the U.S. economy has suffered less than most of Europe.

Free agency has led people into their most productive occupations. It has enabled employers to adjust payroll to reflect their competitive situation. Free agency has enabled the U.S. to lead the developed nations in economic growth and productivity. Even during periods of recession, the ability to adjust employment levels quickly enables employers to respond to conditions. They can keep the company solvent and quickly rehire people when the situation improves. This flexibility will help us remain competitive with developing nations like China and India, who will compete more and more for the higher-paying jobs in the global economy.

Destigmatized

For the generation that grew up in the Great Depression and won World War II, employment was a very different animal than it is today. There was less individuality and more *esprit de corps* then. This was due in no small part to the historic events these people had experienced.

When 25% of the population was out of work, as was the case during the depths of the Great Depression, you took a job, said thank you, kept your mouth shut, kept your shoulder to the wheel, and forgot about self-fulfillment. If your stomach was full, you were better off than most. If you felt like complaining, there were 20 guys waiting to take your place.

World War II required a team thinking we hadn't needed before and haven't seen since. The millions serving in the military certainly had it. They couldn't defeat two powerful enemies on two different fronts unless they put the needs of the country ahead of their own. Those on the home front made sacrifices as well. There was rationing of almost everything. The entire economy was skewed to produce war materiel. There were wage and price freezes in effect, plus many other limitations that would not be tolerated in peacetime.

When this generation went to work after the war, they carried those values and habits into the workplace. They tended to dress alike. They were disciplined. They put the good of the company above their own self-interest. And they stayed loyal to their employer. Leaving one job for another was not a common practice. A person needed a compelling reason (more compelling than a modest raise) to leave a company. Frequent job hoppers were looked at like someone with a disfiguring social disease.

They put in their time, worked their way up the corporate ladder, and retired with a nice pension. Pension is something some of you under 30 may not know. Back in the old days, there were no 401(k) plans. In exchange for years of loyal service, your employer would provide a lifetime of financial support for you and your spouse upon your retirement. It was known as a pension. You couldn't outlive it. It didn't fluctuate with the stock market. In exchange for the best years of your life (25 years was usually the minimum service time to earn one of these pensions), your employer promised an income for you and your spouse for the rest of your lives.

The immobility of the pension also tended to make the worker immobile, too. After a decade or two with an employer, workers would question the wisdom of tossing away a nice retirement income to start again somewhere else. Few situations could justify such a move from a financial standpoint.

Long-time employees were comfortably nestled in their jobs. They would mark time until they hit their magic number, collected their gold watches, and headed off for unlimited fishing. Their productivity might sag in those last years as they set it on cruise control. But an employer was unlikely to fire a long-timer without substantial cause.

The children of these loyalists were the Baby Boomers. They took a different approach. They grew up in an age of affluence and economic security. Because they had never known economic insecurity, they didn't place as high a value on such security as their parents. Baby boomers sought opportunity more than security when they entered the workforce.

When opportunity knocks, you answer. Baby boomers changed jobs, even careers, more than any previous generation had. Part of this practice was a response to the increasing speed of change in the workplace. In addition to sweeping changes brought on by technology, there were also legislated changes such as new anti-discrimination policies. There was also an entry of women into the workplace on an unprecedented scale in history.

At the same time, the corporate perspective of employees was changing. As the economy struggled in the late 1970's and early 80's, companies had to reassess the old notion of lifetime employment. Technology was rendering many jobs obsolete. Competition from outside the U.S. was growing. Pressure from stockholders to improve the bottom line was intense.

Layoffs were becoming commonplace. And it wasn't just the last-hired-first-fired routine. Companies were looking at productivity as the main measure of who got to stay and who had to go. With every round of layoffs, the survivors got more nervous. All the old rules of the workplace seemed to be falling away.

Internal Revenue Code Section 401(k) was introduced by the Revenue Act of 1978. The basics of a 401(k) retirement plan are:

- The employee makes contributions to the plan, which are tax deductible.
- The employer typically matches employee contributions in some ratio.
- The contributions can be invested in stocks, bonds, and mutual funds that provide long-term growth.
- No income tax is due until money comes out of the 401(k).
- The cost is less for the employer, compared to a traditional pension plan.
- The employee can take the money in the 401(k) plan with him/her upon departure from that employer.

Read those last two items again. *The cost is less for the employer.* How long do you think it took for practically every company in America to establish a 401(k) plan for its employees? Corporations hate traditional pension plans because they can't get a good handle on what the cost will be to fund them. Just when the number-crunchers think they have the average life-expectancy and cost of-living increase numbers figured out, there's a spike in inflation or some medical breakthrough increases life spans and throws all their calculations out the window. With a 401(k) plan, the employer can gauge how much they will have to contribute each year, based on employee contributions. They can even make the employer contributions contingent on corporate profitability; they are not on the hook unless the company makes money.

Such a contingency eases the financial pressure on the company. It also provides an incentive for the employees to keep the old noses to the grindstone. In short, **a traditional pension defines the *benefit* the employer must provide, regardless of the cost. With a 401(k), the *contribution* is defined by the employer.** The cost of the 401(k) is controllable and predictable. The pension isn't, which is why the pension in the private sector is now almost extinct.

The second item is *The employee can take the money in the 401(k) plan with him/her upon departure from that employer.* You are no longer tethered to a company in a dead-end job just because you have so much time invested toward a pension that you can't afford to start over somewhere else.

Everything you put into a 401(k) plan is yours right away. Typically, the company contributions have a vesting schedule. Step-vesting is common. You get to keep 20% more of the company contributions each year until you are completely vested.

When you leave the company, you can roll over the proceeds from the 401(k) plan into an IRA. There it will keep doing the same thing it was doing before – growing the funds you will need for retirement. In the meantime, you get yourself enrolled in the 401(k) plan at your new job and keep the ball rolling.

Today, someone with decades of service at one

company is often viewed in the same manner as the job hopper of fifty years ago. Unless they are in the upper echelons of corporate management, the unspoken question seems to be, "What's wrong with that person?"

There's probably nothing wrong with that person. The corporate world needs both types. It needs the long-timers. They provide stability and a sense of corporate culture to all the new, wet-behind-the-ears types. The corporate world also needs the free agents. They need those who are willing to consider making a change under the right circumstances. Those people make a company keep its compensation and work environment up to date and enticing to current and potential employees. The one thing no one needs is a hummingbird.

There's no one less enticing to an employer than someone who is constantly flitting from one job to another. When someone has a pattern of changing jobs like the changing of the seasons, the problem lies with that person, not the mosaic of former employers. If you've had ten different employers in the last five years, the one common factor in all ten cases is you.

Once the pattern is established, the only organizations who hire hummingbirds are the desperate ones. Desperate organizations are not good places to work, so the hummingbird soon leaves, and the downward spiral continues.

Freedom Isn't Free

There is one big difference between professional athletes and the rest of us when it comes to putting ourselves on the open market. It's called a guaranteed contract.

Part of the negotiation for an athlete, in addition to

salary, is the length of the contract. The older the athlete, the less they worry about opportunities and the more they worry about security. (Come to think of it, we all tend to be that way.) The athlete wants to know that if he is injured, or just can't perform at peak level any more, he will still draw a nice paycheck.

The Average Joe gets no such arrangement. Teachers typically sign a one-year contract, but that is done primarily to lock the teacher into a school system, not to guarantee a paycheck despite performance. It's hard to have any leverage when you're an Average Joe.

Increased freedom to move around to find your best place is mostly a good thing. You have a better chance of working in a field for which you have a passion. You have a better chance of getting paid more than if there weren't such freedom of movement. People respect your time more when you're a free agent because they can't control you. You can self-define success. You aren't stigmatized if you change jobs, as long as you don't become a hummingbird. But there's a price to be paid for such opportunity. You are at the mercy of the market. When the economy starts to sputter, you can feel like you're in a rowboat in the middle of the ocean in a hurricane.

Even if the general economy is OK, if your employer is struggling, the first thing they will look to do is "trim the fat." Very often lean muscle is trimmed from the payroll as well. It doesn't much matter which you are if you've been trimmed. You still have to go find another job.

Sometimes the economy is good, your company is doing fine, but they keep pushing the employees harder anyway. While it has become easier for an employee to leave for other opportunities, it has also become easier for employers to dismiss workers. They typically have to show just cause, but that interpretation is fairly liberal most times. It's to be expected that an employer will try to wring as much productivity out of employees as possible. You just need to know when it's gone too far and what to do at that point.

The main thing to remember in the era of free agency is **you must constantly prove your worth to your employer, just as they must prove their worth to you.**

6,000,000 MINUTES ON THE CLOCK

6,000,000 MINUTES ON THE CLOCK

WHO DO YOU THINK YOU ARE?

Question: Who is responsible for the Beatles, night baseball, *The Godfather*, and the "crawler" at the bottom of the screen on CNN? Answer: Thomas Edison

Four of Edison's most well-known inventions are the phonograph, the electric light, the movie projector, and the stock ticker. Without those inventions, the above list doesn't happen.

Perhaps more than anyone else in history, Thomas Edison seems the perfect fit for the work he did. He held 1,093 patents on his inventions. He had so many things going on at once, he had to start a company to keep everything running smoothly. We know it as General Electric.

Thomas Edison was known for his work habits. Twenty-hour workdays and hundred-hour workweeks were common. Edison worked an estimated 14,000,000 minutes in his life. (12 hour days; 6 day weeks; 50 weeks/year; 65 years).

Edison famously said, "Genius is 1% inspiration, and 99% perspiration." He recognized the sweat of the brain and the brow were necessary for success.

How could someone work like that for more than sixty years without burning out? Edison loved his work so much he didn't *want* to do anything else. Edison spent the better part of two years creating a practical light bulb. He tested thousands of filaments (over six thousand plant filaments alone) before finding one that would last. It may seem obsessive-compulsive to most of us, but look at the results. Turn on a light first; you'll see better.

6,000,000 MINUTES ON THE CLOCK

Edison is the poster boy for what kind of success is possible when the right person is in the right job. Edison points out in his biography that it isn't hard work that kills someone (he died at 84); it's stress and worry. Few things are more worrisome than wondering if you're wasting your life doing the wrong work.

There are countless ways that people define work. Most of them involve an exchange of time and talent for treasure. For the moment, exclude money from the following definition: work is doing what you *have* to do; play is doing what you *want* to do.

If work is defined as doing what you have to do, then many of the things we have to do qualify as work even though we don't get paid to do them. On the other hand, if we get paid for doing things we want to do, it's like getting paid to play. Given the choice, would you rather be like Edison and spend 14,000,000 minutes of your life getting paid to do things you want to do? Or would you rather spend 6,000,000 minutes doing things you have to do? The second choice is shorter; it only feels longer.

Edison invented many things, but his first and most important invention was his career. Then as now, there were no colleges where one could learn to become an inventor. Edison learned at an early age what he loved to do and what he was good at. One of the reasons he loved what he did was he could see the benefits to mankind that his work produced. He invented a career that enabled him to do what he did best and that gave people many ways to make their lives better.

People who are doing work that's ill-suited for them are easy to spot – they look like a square peg in a round hole. It's no fun feeling like that square peg, getting pounded into that round hole day after day. It's no fun for the hole, either. When someone is in the wrong job, the employee, the employer, and the customers all suffer. It's a lose-lose-lose proposition.

For better or worse, much of our identity is connected to our work. When you meet someone for the first time, one of the first questions people ask is "What do you do for a living?" Many of us strive to have an impressive answer to that question, even if the most correct answer might be, "I'm a square peg in a round hole." If you based your career choice on impressing others or money (often the same thing), then being a square peg in a round hole is on you.

Here's a little test to see how well your job fits you. Just answer the questions honestly; there are no right or wrong answers.

- As you are getting ready for work, what are you feeling – anticipation, dread, or just apathy?
- Is your work a source of your energy or a consumer of your energy?
- Do you feel you are making a contribution to your organization and to the world at large?
- Do you feel that your contribution is recognized, at least within your organization, if not by the world at large?
- Is there a sense of pride when you describe what you do for a living?
- Is your level of happiness in your job as high as your level of success in your job?
- Do you support and respect your employer and believe in their mission statement?
- Can you see yourself in this same line of work in ten years? In twenty? If not, why not?
- Ignoring your immediate financial situation, would a 15% pay cut make you leave your current line of work?

6,000,000 MINUTES ON THE CLOCK

- If you-in-the-present went back to visit you-as-a-ten-year-old and described what you do for a living, how would you-as-a-ten-year-old react?
- Would you want your child to be in your line of work when he/she grows up?

Before we go any further, the purpose of this book is not to create dissatisfaction for anyone with his/her job or career choices. That would do a disservice to the reader and would be counterproductive.

For those who are already dissatisfied with their current work, you want to recognize *why* you are dissatisfied and take steps to find satisfaction. (By the way, satisfaction is what *you*, not someone else, define it to be.) The steps may involve a change of employers or even careers, but not necessarily.

Many of you may be quite satisfied with your work, but for some reason you can't see it. Maybe peers keep telling you that you should be doing something else. Maybe you think you should go where the pay is the highest. Maybe your parents haven't quite embraced your chosen calling. Maybe you're just in a spot right now where the cons are more obvious than the pros. This book may help you recognize that you are in the right place. As a result, you may become happier and more successful. If so, this book is useful to you, too.

Remember most of all, **you change careers to fit you; you don't change who you are to fit a career.** Careers are like clothes. You may have to try several on until you find the right size and style that's a perfect fit. Also, your clothes change as your style and size change; your career should, too. With clothes and careers, we work within what works for us.

6,000,000 MINUTES ON THE CLOCK

The Sweet 16

I am an ENFJ, along with people like Pope John Paul II, Abraham Lincoln, Ronald Reagan, Barack Obama, and Oprah Winfrey. My kinship to these people is based on the Jung Typology Test. Carl Jung (1875-1961) was an eminent Swiss psychiatrist and the founder of analytical psychology. Among other things, Jung gave us the concept of the introvert and the extrovert.

According to Jung's typology, every individual can be classified using these three criteria:
- Extroversion – Introversion
- Sensing – Intuition
- Thinking – Feeling

Isabel Briggs-Myers (1897-1980), a noted American psychiatrist, added a fourth criterion:
- Judging – Perceiving

Isabel, along with her mother, Katharine Briggs, developed the Myers-Briggs Type Indicator (MBTI). The MBTI is not a test, in that tests have right and wrong answers. The MBTI is a personality inventory in which there are no right or wrong answers, and it is designed to measure how people perceive the world and make decisions.

Taking any personality evaluation online can help assess your personality traits, but the results of such evaluations should not be the basis for making changes in careers, relationships, or even investments. Further evaluation by trained professionals would be necessary before making any major life changes.

Humanmetrics.com definition of the four criteria follows:
- "The first criterion, **Extroversion - Introversion** defines the source and direction of energy expression

for a person. The extrovert has a source and direction of energy expression mainly in the external world while the introvert has a source of energy mainly in the internal world.
- The second criterion, **Sensing - iNtuition** defines the method of information perception by a person. Sensing means that a person believes mainly information he or she receives directly from the external world. Intuition means that a person believes mainly information he/she receives from the internal or imaginative world.
- The third criterion, **Thinking - Feeling** defines how the person processes information. Thinking means that a person makes a decision mainly through logic. Feeling means that, as a rule, he/she makes a decision based on emotion.
- The fourth criterion, **Judging - Perceiving** defines how a person implements the information he/she has processed. Judging means that a person organizes all his/her life events and acts strictly according to his/her plans. Perceiving means that he/she is inclined to improvise and seek alternatives."

MYERS-BRIGGS TYPE INDICATOR
Four Criteria — Sixteen Personality Types

E — Source of energy — I
Extraversion / Introversion

S — Way of gathering information — N
Sensing / iNtuition

T — Decision making — F
Thinking / Feeling

J — How you relate to the external world — P
Judgment / Perception

"Try your traits before trying fate." -Humanmetrics.com

6,000,000 MINUTES ON THE CLOCK

Different combinations of these criteria determine a personality type. There are sixteen types. Every type has a name, based on the combination of criteria. The sixteen types are listed below, with the percentage of the U.S. population that falls into each type:

ISTJ-11.6%	ISFJ-13.8%	INFJ-1.5%	INTJ-2.1%
ISTP-5.4%	ISFP-8.8%	INFP-4.3%	INTP-3.3%
ESTP-4.3%	ESFP-8.5%	ENFP-8.1%	ENTP-3.2%
ESTJ-8.7%	ESFJ-12.3%	ENFJ-2.4%	ENTJ-1.8%

Here is more detailed information about these eight different personality traits and the people who possess them:

EXTROVERTS:
- Are energized by being with other people
- Like being the center of attention
- Act, then think
- Tend to think out loud
- Are easier to read and know, share personal information freely
- Talk more than listen
- Communicate with enthusiasm
- Respond quickly, enjoy a fast pace
- Prefer breadth to depth

INTROVERTS:
- Are energized by spending time alone
- Avoid being the center of attention
- Think, then act
- Think things through inside their head
- Are more private, prefer to share personal information with a select few
- Listen more than talk

6,000,000 MINUTES ON THE CLOCK

- Keep their enthusiasm to themselves;
- Respond after taking the time to think things through, enjoy a slower pace
- Prefer depth to breadth

SENSORS:
- Trust what is certain and concrete
- Like new ideas only if they have practical application
- Value realism and common sense
- Like to use and hone established skills
- Tend to be specific and literal, give detailed descriptions
- Present information in a step-by-step manner
- Are oriented to the present

INTUITIVES:
- Trust inspiration and inference
- Like new ideas and concepts for their own sake
- Value imagination and innovation
- Like to learn new skills, get bored easily after mastering skills
- Tend to be general and figurative, use metaphors and analogies
- Present information through leaps, in a roundabout manner
- Are oriented toward the future

THINKERS:
- Step back and apply impersonal analysis to problems
- Value logic, justice, and fairness; one standard for all
- Naturally see flaws and tend to be critical
- May be seen as heartless, insensitive and uncaring
- Consider it more important to be truthful than tactful

6,000,000 MINUTES ON THE CLOCK

FEELERS:
- Step forward, consider the effect of actions on others
- Value empathy and harmony
- Naturally like to please others, show appreciation easily
- May be seen as overemotional, illogical, and weak
- Consider it important to be tactful as well as truthful

JUDGERS:
- Are happiest after decisions have been made
- Have a work ethic - work first, play later
- Set goals and work toward achieving them on time
- Prefer knowing what they are getting into
- Emphasize completion of the task
- Derive satisfaction from finishing projects
- See time as a finite resource and take deadlines seriously

PERCEIVERS:
- Are happiest leaving their options open
- Have a play ethic - play now, work later
- Change goals as new information becomes available
- Like adapting to new situations
- Emphasize how a task is completed
- Derive satisfaction from starting projects
- See time as a renewable resource

The following synopsis of each of the sixteen personality types is excerpted from Introduction to Type by Isabel Briggs Myers, published by CPP. Inc.:

ISTJ
Quiet, serious, earn success by thoroughness and dependability. Practical, matter-of-fact, realistic, and

responsible. Decide logically what should be done and work toward it steadily, regardless of distractions. Take pleasure in making everything orderly and organized – their work, their home, their life. Value traditions and loyalty.

ISFJ
Quiet, friendly, responsible, and conscientious. Committed and steady in meeting their obligations. Thorough, painstaking, and accurate. Loyal, considerate, notice and remember specifics about people who are important to them, concerned with how others feel. Strive to create an orderly and harmonious environment at work and at home.

INFJ
Seek meaning and connection in ideas, relationships, and material possessions. Want to understand what motivates people and are insightful about others. Conscientious and committed to their firm values. Develop a clear vision about how best to serve the common good. Organized and decisive in implementing their vision.

INTJ
Have original minds and great drive for implementing their ideas and achieving their goals. Quickly see patterns in external events and develop long-range explanatory perspectives. When committed, organize a job and carry it through. Skeptical and independent, have high standards of competence and performance – for themselves and others.

ISTP
Tolerant and flexible, quiet observers until a problem

appears, then act quickly to find workable solutions. Analyze what makes things work and readily get through large amounts of data to isolate the core of practical problems. Interested in cause and effect, organize facts using logical principles, value efficiency.

ISFP
Quiet, friendly, sensitive, and kind. Enjoy the present moment, what's going on around them. Like to have their own space and to work within their own time frame. Loyal and committed to their values and to people who are important to them. Dislike disagreements and conflicts, do not force their opinions or values on others.

INFP
Idealistic, loyal to their values and to people who are important to them. Want an external life that is congruent with their values. Curious, quick to see possibilities, can be catalysts for implementing ideas. Seek to understand people and to help them fulfill their potential. Adaptable, flexible, and accepting unless a value is threatened.

INTP
Seek to develop logical explanations for everything that interests them. Theoretical and abstract, interested more in ideas than in social interaction. Quiet, contained, flexible, and adaptable. Have unusual ability to focus in depth to solve problems in their area of interest. Skeptical, sometimes critical, always analytical.

ESTP
Flexible and tolerant, they take a pragmatic approach

focused on immediate results. Theories and conceptual explanations bore them – they want to act energetically to solve the problem. Focus on the here-and-now, spontaneous, enjoy each moment that they can be active with others. Enjoy material comforts and style. Learn best through doing.

ESFP
Outgoing, friendly, and accepting. Exuberant lovers of life, people, and material comforts. Enjoy working with others to make things happen. Bring common sense and a realistic approach to their work, and make work fun. Flexible and spontaneous, adapt readily to new people and environments. Learn best by trying a new skill with other people.

ENFP
Warmly enthusiastic and imaginative. See life as full of possibilities. Make connections between events and information very quickly, and confidently proceed based on the patterns they see. Want a lot of affirmation from others, and readily give appreciation and support. Spontaneous and flexible, often rely on their ability to improvise and their verbal fluency.

ENTP
Quick, ingenious, stimulating, alert, and outspoken. Resourceful in solving new and challenging problems. Adept at generating conceptual possibilities and then analyzing them strategically. Good at reading other people. Bored by routine, will seldom do the same thing the same way, apt to turn to one new interest after another.

6,000,000 MINUTES ON THE CLOCK

ESTJ
Practical, realistic, matter-of-fact. Decisive, quickly move to implement decisions. Organize projects and people to get things done, focus on getting results in the most efficient way possible. Take care of routine details. Have a clear set of logical standards, systematically follow them and want others to also. Forceful in implementing their plans.

ESFJ
Warmhearted, conscientious, and cooperative. Want harmony in their environment, work with determination to establish it. Like to work with others to complete tasks accurately and on time. Loyal, follow through even in small matters. Notice what others need in their day-by-day lives and try to provide it. Want to be appreciated for who they are and for what they contribute.

ENFJ
Warm, empathetic, responsive, and responsible. Highly attuned to the emotions, needs, and motivations of others. Find potential in everyone, want to help others fulfill their potential. May act as catalysts for individual and group growth. Loyal, responsive to praise and criticism. Sociable, facilitate others in a group, and provide inspiring leadership.

ENTJ
Frank, decisive, assume leadership readily. Quickly see illogical and inefficient procedures and policies, develop and implement comprehensive systems to solve organizational problems. Enjoy long-term planning and goal setting. Usually well informed, well read, enjoy

expanding their knowledge and passing it on to others. Forceful in presenting their ideas.

Keep in mind that your answers may vary depending on your situation or mood when you take the test, so don't feel like you are locked into a personality type based on a single taking of the test. Below are the questions. They all require either a Yes or No answer:

- You are almost never late for your appointments.
- You like to be engaged in an active and fast-paced job.
- You enjoy having a wide circle of acquaintances.
- You feel involved when watching TV soaps.
- You are usually the first to react to a sudden event: the telephone ringing or unexpected question
- You are more interested in a general idea than in the details of its realization.
- You tend to be unbiased even if this might endanger your good relations with people.
- Strict observance of the established rules is likely to prevent a good outcome.
- It's difficult to get you excited.
- It is in your nature to assume responsibility.
- You often think about humankind and its destiny.
- You believe the best decision is one that can be easily changed.
- Objective criticism is always useful in any activity.
- You prefer to act immediately rather than speculate about various options.
- You trust reason rather than feelings.
- You are inclined to rely more on improvisation than on careful planning.
- You spend your leisure time actively socializing with a group of people, attending parties, shopping, etc.

6,000,000 MINUTES ON THE CLOCK

- You usually plan your actions in advance.
- Your actions are frequently influenced by emotions.
- You are a person somewhat reserved and distant in communication.
- You know how to put every minute of your time to good purpose.
- You readily help people while asking nothing in return.
- You often contemplate about the complexity of life.
- After prolonged socializing you feel you need to get away and be alone.
- You often do jobs in a hurry.
- You easily see the general principle behind specific occurrences.
- You frequently and easily express your feelings and emotions.
- You find it difficult to speak loudly.
- You get bored if you have to read theoretical books.
- You tend to sympathize with other people.
- You value justice higher than mercy.
- You rapidly get involved in social life at a new workplace.
- The more people with whom you speak, the better you feel.
- You tend to rely on your experience rather than on theoretical alternatives.
- You like to keep a check on how things are progressing.
- You easily empathize with the concerns of other people.
- Often you prefer to read a book than go to a party.
- You enjoy being at the center of events in which other people are directly involved.

6,000,000 MINUTES ON THE CLOCK

- You are more inclined to experiment than to follow familiar approaches.
- You avoid being bound by obligations.
- You are strongly touched by the stories about people's troubles.
- Deadlines seem to you to be of relative, rather than absolute importance.
- You prefer to isolate yourself from outside noises.
- It's essential for you to try things with your own hands.
- You think that almost everything can be analyzed.
- You do your best to complete a task on time.
- You take pleasure in putting things in order.
- You feel at ease in a crowd.
- You have good control over your desires and temptations.
- You easily understand new theoretical principles.
- The process of searching for a solution is more important to you than the solution itself.
- You usually place yourself nearer to the side than in the center of the room.
- When solving a problem you would rather follow a familiar approach than seek a new one.
- You try to stand firmly by your principles.
- A thirst for adventure is close to your heart.
- You prefer meeting in small groups to interaction with lots of people.
- When considering a situation you pay more attention to the current situation and less to a possible sequence of events.
- You consider the scientific approach to be the best.
- You find it difficult to talk about your feelings.
- You often spend time thinking of how things could be improved.

6,000,000 MINUTES ON THE CLOCK

- Your decisions are based more on the feelings of a moment than on the careful planning.
- You prefer to spend your leisure time alone or relaxing in a tranquil family atmosphere.
- You feel more comfortable sticking to conventional ways.
- You are easily affected by strong emotions.
- You are always looking for opportunities.
- Your desk, workbench etc. is usually neat and orderly.
- As a rule, current preoccupations worry you more than future plans.
- You get pleasure from solitary walks.
- It is easy for you to communicate in social situations.
- You are consistent in your habits.
- You willingly involve yourself in matters which engage your sympathies.
- You easily perceive various ways in which events could develop.

Because everyone ends up in one of only sixteen types, people within a type can still vary widely in terms of their overall personalities. There are some 42 million ISFJs in the U.S. alone, and they will hardly be clones of each other. We can, however, look at the eight personality traits to get an indication of how someone who possesses those traits is likely to act in various situations

It can be easy to look at these personality traits and stereotype people who possess them, usually in a negative way. It can be easy to assume that extroverts are loudmouths, that feelers are bleeding hearts, or that perceivers are slackers. Of course, we will not have negative stereotypes of the traits *we* possess. Since fifteen of sixteen personality types are *not* you, you do yourself a disservice to create too many negative stereotypes of such a large group of others.

Extroverts tend to act before thinking, which can lead to some regrettable decisions regarding their health and wealth. Their bias for action also puts them in the lead in many new ventures. Extroverts are more likely to be in on the ground floor of some game-changing new products and services. Extroverts are like the baseball player who leads the league in home runs *and* strikeouts.

Extroverts talk more than they listen, so they may be deaf to warnings issued by others. They can also turn a deaf ear to the naysayers who say nay to some very good ideas. Their filters are often less discerning between good and bad ideas than the extrovert imagines them to be.

Extroverts enjoy a fast pace and are quick responders. Extroverts prefer breadth to depth and are likely to have their thumbs in many pies and many irons in the fire. Extroverts are likely to buy investments on the high-risk-high-return end of the spectrum.

Because they seek out social relationships more than introverts, extroverts are more likely to reap the benefits of those relationships, such as a greater sense of well-being and lower levels of stress.

When you think of introverts, you may picture an economics professor with a bow tie and sweater vest, working on a new method to calculate standard deviation or something. Such an introvert would be more interested in developing a new economic theory than in discussing it on CNN. Introverts think first and then act. They are slow and deliberate. It is more important for them to get it right than to get it right now.

Introverts listen more than they talk. They will gather as much information as possible in order to make the most informed decision possible. This trait can cause them to develop information overload, which can lead to decision paralysis.

Introverts prefer depth to breadth. They are likely to hold fewer stocks in their portfolio than extroverts, but they will have more in-depth knowledge of the companies they own.

Introverts won't hit a lot of home runs; they won't strike out much, either. They will not get rich overnight; they may get rich over time. Introverts do not necessarily favor security over opportunity, nor do extroverts necessarily favor the opposite.

Research shows that the brains of introverts are more active than the brains of extroverts. Introverts prefer to exercise their minds while extroverts prefer to exercise their jaws. There is a bias in professional and lay circles that extroverts are happier than introverts. Studies have led to this conclusion, though the testing methods may favor the way extroverts choose to express happiness.

The worst aspect of introversion is that the introvert may feel pressure to become an extrovert. There is nothing wrong with preferring to read a book than to go to a party. Introverts try to become extroverts far more than extroverts try to become introverts. This disparity may explain in part the lower stress levels of extroverts; they're not trying to be something they aren't.

Introverts tend to favor quality over quantity and specialization over generalization, as compared to extroverts. Introverts are more likely to practice moderation in their habits, which can serve them well. Introverts prefer to do a few things and to do them well, which can lead to a greater sense of accomplishment. Introverts are less likely to need the approval of others to boost their self-esteem.

6,000,000 MINUTES ON THE CLOCK

Sensors trust what is certain and concrete, though they may eventually find little to trust in a world filled with uncertainty. Once sensors lose trust in something, it may never return.

Sensors are not likely to be on the vanguard of something new, due to their preference for using established skills and ideas that have an immediate practical application. They will be more conservative in most life choices, including how they save, spend, and invest their money. Sensors are specific and literal, which means you are not likely to convince them of something by appealing to their imagination.

Sensors are oriented to the present, which is not to say that they don't plan for the future. Their vision of the future is grounded in the present, so they plan for the future based on what they are certain of in the present. One drawback to this strategy is that the constant change of modern life means that what is certain today may not be at all certain in the future. During stable times, sensors fare quite well. Rapid change requires adaptability, with which sensors often need help.

Because sensors are more oriented to the present, it can be difficult to get them to imagine themselves as old when they are young. A forty-year-old sensor may have difficulty imagining how the habits of today will affect him/her in three decades. Aging well is a process of adaptation, which is not a strong suit of the sensor.

Intuitives make up the great majority of entrepreneurs. An entrepreneur is not someone looking to make a quick buck in a business; it's someone who loves to take an idea and make it a reality. True entrepreneurs are more missionary than mercenary. Being intuitive is a great asset in that line of work.

6,000,000 MINUTES ON THE CLOCK

Intuitives like new ideas for their own sake, so they may find themselves investing in concepts that turn out to have no economic benefit. Because they are open to new ideas and concepts, they are also more likely to see the potential in an idea before everyone else does, causing them to be the leaders in new fields. Imagination and innovation are highly valued, so the best and brightest are drawn to work with intuitives.

Intuitives are oriented to the future, which is why so many of their ventures pay off. They see now what becomes obvious to the rest of us only much later. The downside to such a future orientation is a lack of attention to the present. More often than not, the Intuitive is derailed not by a bad idea, but by inattention to present realities, which can upset the best-laid plans.

Although intuitives are oriented to the future, that doesn't mean they are taking good care of themselves in the present. The focus on the future often means the drudgery of the present is avoided, and a good future does require a certain measure of drudgery in the present.

Thinkers are very left-brain people. Their minds are like high-powered computers. There are some paradoxes with Thinkers. They value justice and fairness, but are viewed as heartless and insensitive. They view themselves as holding on to principles; others view them as rigid and unfeeling.

Thinkers are capable of stepping back and applying impersonal analysis to problems. This trait makes them very good at getting to the unvarnished truth. When something is going wrong in a business, Thinkers are the ones who will roll up their sleeves and figure out what needs to be done. Because they value truth more than tact, when they report their findings to management, they may do so in a way that actually gets in the way of needed reform.

Because Thinkers are more accurately *critical* thinkers, they are good at finding flaws. This perspective also tends to make Thinkers more pessimistic than the general population; they will see the glass as half-empty, as well as dirty and chipped. A pessimistic outlook combined with a frustration over the imperfections of life can inhibit Thinkers from taking long-term risks for long-term rewards.

Thinkers are good at putting the brakes on activities that are going too fast. Brakes alone don't go anywhere, though. Thinkers need relationships with those who move forward to avoid stagnation.

Thinkers will take care of themselves if it is logical to do so. They will be motivated by statistics on heart disease, not by a commercial for an energy drink. The natural pessimism of thinkers can be more than a liability in the present (pessimism is far more stressful than optimism). That pessimism can make it harder to imagine a future that is worth making any sacrifices for in the present.

Feelers are team players. They value empathy and harmony and are always considerate of the feelings of others. They will not gain at the expense of others and may be more inclined to be taken advantage of by others. In a competitive environment, Feelers will have a problem, and they will not choose a tournament-style conflict if there are alternatives.

Because they understand the human aspect in any situation better than most, Feelers are better equipped to motivate people to action. Thinkers may be great at knowing which direction people should go, but it usually takes Feelers to actually get the people moving in that direction.

Feelers are cooperative, not competitive. Because of this nature, Feelers may not fare as well in the short term. However, in the long term, Feelers will fare better than most others because the more long-term the goals are, the more cooperation, rather than competition, is needed to achieve them. Feelers are not combative, and they might lose many battles. They are more likely to end up winning a war, though.

Judgers are not likely to end up being supported by their children in their old age. They are very good at setting goals and working toward achieving them by the deadline. Judgers are motivated by the satisfaction they get from completing a project. Nothing makes them happier than setting a goal of being financially independent by a certain date and actually achieving that independence.

Judgers believe in business before pleasure. They will make sure that all financial obligations (including obligations to themselves) are met before they spend money on items like vacations or luxury cars. They also are likely to succeed in starting their own businesses because they are more likely to make the sacrifices necessary in the early years to enable a business to succeed in the long run.

Judgers are deadline-conscious and so value time as a finite, exhaustible resource. This trait is mostly useful because it encourages careful use of time. Judgers can also put unnecessary pressure on themselves to complete a task on time, which can sometimes result in compromises in quality, or even major errors in judgment. Strict adherence to deadlines can confine Judgers when flexibility may be the more valuable trait.

6,000,000 MINUTES ON THE CLOCK

Perceivers are recognized for their flexibility and adaptability, but they can sometimes resemble a boat with a sail and no rudder. The desire to keep their options open can cause them to avoid setting goals.

Perceivers enjoy the mechanics of completing a task more than the accomplishment of the task itself. They are good at developing the tactics necessary to implement the strategy that was created by others. They can adapt as new information becomes available, though they are not likely to be the ones generating that new information.

Perceivers see time as a renewable resource, so they are prone to find themselves out of time. For them, it's pleasure before business. Perceivers may be more inclined to work to a much older age, in part because they still see themselves as young and vital, but also because they may have procrastinated in taking concrete steps to enable them to afford to retire. In the Aesop's fable, the ants would have been Judgers; the grasshopper, a perceiver.

Personality evaluations like the MBTI can be helpful in assessing your strengths and weaknesses. Because it is impossible for us to be objective about our own strengths and weaknesses, the MBTI can make us aware of such traits. Awareness can help you better utilize your strengths, while enabling you to get help from others who are strong where you may be weak.

There is no ideal personality type. When you read the characteristics of the eight different personality traits, it can be tempting to think that a certain combination is the magic formula for career success. Because every human is unique, no one possesses these personality traits in the exact same combination as anyone else. We are like snowflakes in that respect; the ingredients may be simple, but the product is endlessly varied.

The MBTI can be very helpful in assessing your strengths and weaknesses to help you align your career path with your personality. If you are in a job that doesn't mesh with your personality, you aren't going to be very good at it. If you aren't very good at your job, you aren't likely to be happy or healthy, and you aren't likely to be well paid for it, either.

Personality evaluations can help you find a career that better suits your personality and your strengths, which should enable you to do a better job and make more money. More importantly, getting into a career that fits your personality will greatly increase your chances for happiness on the job, as well as success on the job. You may have spent years trying to make yourself fit a job. Finding out your personality type can enable you to find a job that fits you instead. Since you will spend some 100,000 hours of your life on work-related activities, you should do everything you can to make sure you spend that time in the right place, not as a square peg in a round hole.

Finally, if you are going to take an MBTI or similar evaluation, wait several days after reading this chapter. The information here may influence your answers and turn you into someone you're not. Also, take the evaluation when you are in a good frame of mind, without stress or distractions. You will get a more accurate result, which is what you want.

6,000,000 MINUTES ON THE CLOCK

A Little Temperamental

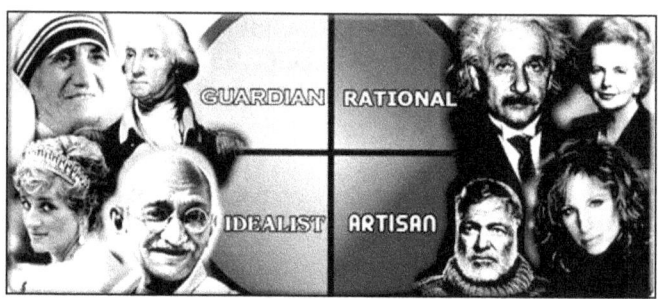

Keirsey Temperament Sorter is in the same vein as MBTI/Jung. This "personality instrument" classifies people into one of four temperaments – artisan, guardian, rational, or idealist. KTS-II, as it's called, can help clarify and reinforce results from the MBTI. It can be taken at www.keirsey.com, which provides the following details.

Temperament is a configuration of observable personality traits, such as habits of communication, patterns of action, and sets of characteristic attitudes, values, and talents. It also encompasses personal needs, the kinds of contributions that individuals make in the workplace, and the roles they play in society. Dr. David Keirsey has identified mankind's four basic temperaments as the Artisan, the Guardian, the Rational, and the Idealist.

Each temperament has its own unique qualities and shortcomings, strengths and challenges. What accounts for these differences? To use the idea of Temperament most effectively, it is important to understand that the four temperaments are not simply arbitrary collections of characteristics, but spring from an interaction of the two basic dimensions of human behavior: our communication and our action, our words and our deeds, or, simply, ***what we say*** and ***what we do***.

Communication: Concrete vs. Abstract

First, people naturally think and talk about what they are interested in, and if you listen carefully to people's conversations, you find two broad but distinct areas of subject matter.

Some people talk primarily about the external, concrete world of everyday reality: facts and figures, work and play, home and family, news, sports and weather -- all the who-what-when-where-and how much's of life.

Other people talk primarily about the internal, abstract world of ideas: theories and conjectures, dreams and philosophies, beliefs and fantasies --all the why's, if's, and what-might-be's of life.

At times, of course, everyone addresses both sorts of topics, but in their daily lives, and for the most part, **Concrete** people talk about *reality*, while **Abstract** people talk about *ideas*.

Action: Utilitarian vs. Cooperative

Second, at every turn people are trying to accomplish their goals, and if you watch closely how people go about their business, you see that there are two fundamentally opposite types of action.

Some people act primarily in a utilitarian or pragmatic manner, that is, they do what gets results, what achieves their objectives as effectively or efficiently as possible, and only afterwards do they check to see if they are observing the rules or going through proper channels.

6,000,000 MINUTES ON THE CLOCK

Other people act primarily in a cooperative or socially acceptable manner, that is, they try to do the right thing, in keeping with agreed upon social rules, conventions, and codes of conduct, and only later do they concern themselves with the effectiveness of their actions.

These two ways of acting can overlap, but as they lead their lives, **Utilitarian** people instinctively, and for the most part do what *works*, while **Cooperative** people do what's *right*.

The Four Temperaments

- As *Concrete Cooperators*, **Guardians** speak mostly of their duties and responsibilities, of what they can keep an eye on and take good care of, and they're careful to obey the laws, follow the rules, and respect the rights of others.
- As *Abstract Cooperators*, **Idealists** speak mostly of what they hope for and imagine might be possible for people, and they want to act in good conscience, always trying to reach their goals without compromising their personal code of ethics.
- As *Concrete Utilitarians*, **Artisans** speak mostly about what they see right in front of them, about what they can get their hands on, and they will do whatever works, whatever gives them a quick, effective payoff, even if they have to bend the rules.
- As *Abstract Utilitarians*, **Rationals** speak mostly of what new problems intrigue them and what new solutions they envision, and always pragmatic, they act as efficiently as possible to achieve their objectives, ignoring arbitrary rules and conventions if need be.

6,000,000 MINUTES ON THE CLOCK

The 4 Temperaments

Guardian
Supervisor (ESTJ)   Inspector (ISTJ)
Provider (ESFJ)   Protector (ISFJ)

Artisan
Promoter (ESTP)   Crafter (ISTP)
Performer (ESFP)   Composer (ISFP)

Idealist
Teacher (ENFJ)   Counselor (INFJ)
Champion (ENFP)   Healer (INFP)

Rational
Field Marshal (ENTJ) Mastermind (INTJ)
Inventor (ENTP)   Architect (INTP)

The Big Five

In psychology, the **Big Five personality traits** are five broad domains or dimensions of personality that are used to describe human personality, the five-factor model (FFM). The five factors are openness, conscientiousness, extroversion, agreeableness, and neuroticism. The acronym commonly used to refer to the five traits collectively is OCEAN. Beneath each global factor, a cluster of correlated and more specific primary factors are found; for example, extroversion includes such related qualities as gregariousness, assertiveness, excitement seeking, warmth, activity, and positive emotions.

The Big Five model is able to account for different traits in personality without overlapping. Empirical research has shown that the Big Five personality traits show consistency in interviews, self-descriptions and observations. Moreover, this five-factor structure seems to be found across a wide range of participants of different ages and of different cultures.

A summary of the factors of the Big Five and their constituent traits, such that they form the acronym OCEAN:

Openness to Experience
(*inventive/curious* vs. *consistent/cautious*)
Appreciation for art, emotion, adventure, unusual ideas, curiosity, and variety of experience. Openness reflects the degree of intellectual curiosity, creativity and a preference for novelty and variety a person has. It is also described as the extent to which a person is imaginative or independent, and depicts a personal preference for a variety of activities over a strict routine. Some disagreement remains about how to interpret the openness factor, which is sometimes called "intellect" rather than openness to experience.

Conscientiousness
(*efficient/organized* vs. *easy-going/careless*)
A tendency to be organized and dependable, show self-discipline, act dutifully, aim for achievement, and prefer planned rather than spontaneous behavior.

Extroversion
(*outgoing/energetic* vs. *solitary/reserved*)
Energy, positive emotions, assurgency, assertiveness, sociability and the tendency to seek stimulation in the company of others, and talkativeness.

Agreeableness
(*friendly/compassionate* vs. *analytical/detached*)
A tendency to be compassionate and cooperative rather than suspicious and antagonistic towards others. It is

also a measure of one's trusting and helpful nature, and whether a person is generally well tempered or not.

Neuroticism
(*sensitive/nervous* vs. *secure/confident*)
The tendency to experience unpleasant emotions easily, such as anger, anxiety, depression, and vulnerability. Neuroticism also refers to the degree of emotional stability and impulse control and is sometimes referred to by its low pole, "emotional stability".

Psychology Today's website enables you to take a 10-minute, 25-question test to assess your Big Five personality traits.

The Big M.O.

While personality tests like MBTI and Keirsey can tell you what you want to do, the **Kolbe A Index/Instinct Test** is designed to tell you what you *will* or *won't do*. It evaluates methods of operation based on natural instincts. This test enables the right person, the right project, and the right team to match up. It can be taken at www.kolbe.com.

While MBTI and Keirsey are useful for individuals looking for a better analysis of their personality, Kolbe is used by organizations in both hiring evaluations and in forming teams of compatible and complementary workers. Kolbe's web site touts the RightFit evaluation thusly:

> *RightFit is Kolbe's statistically proven hiring tool that helps companies screen and select the best job applicants. Instead of guessing how well a prospective employee will perform, RightFit helps you identify the required methods of operation, or*

profile, of the ideal candidate. The software then ranks each candidate on an "A" to "F" scale based on how well their individual instincts compare to the requirements for success in a given role. RightFit can also be used to select individuals who match the methods of proven high-performers, as well as individuals who can fill a critical gap on a team.

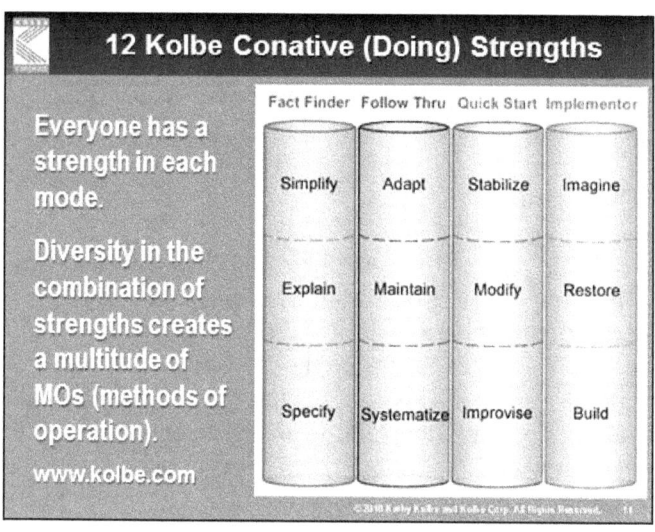

There are four universal human instincts used in creative problem solving. These instincts are not measurable. However, the observable acts derived from them can be identified and quantified by the Kolbe A Index. These instinct-driven behaviors are represented in the four Kolbe Action Modes:

- **Fact Finder** - the instinctive way we gather and share information.

6,000,000 MINUTES ON THE CLOCK

- **Follow Thru** - the instinctive way we arrange and design.
- **Quick Start** - the instinctive way we deal with risk and uncertainty.
- **Implementor** - the instinctive way we handle space and tangibles.

The Kolbe A Index result is a graphical representation of an individual's instinctive method of operation, or modus operandi (M.O.). The numbers in each Action Mode represent different points on a continuum, rather than relative values. Each point on the continuum indicates a positive trait. There is no such thing as a negative or "bad" Kolbe Index result.

You're Such a Character!

Martin Seligman and Chris Peterson are pioneers in the area of positive psychology. For decades, psychology has been focused to the point of obsession on the negative aspects of human personality. Seligman and Peterson have been working to shift that focus to understanding the upper reaches of human health, talent, and possibility.

As their first step in this process, Seligman and Peterson scoured every list of virtues they could find, from religious teachings to the Boy Scout Oath. They discovered that six broad virtues appeared on nearly every list: wisdom, courage, humanity, justice, temperance, and transcendence (the ability to forge connections to something beyond the self). The value of this list of six virtues is as an organizing framework for more specific *strengths of character*. There are several paths to each virtue, and different cultures vary in the degree to which they value each path. The value of the classifications is as a guide to specific means of growth toward widely valued ends, without insisting that any one way is mandatory or even best.

Seligman and Peterson suggest there are twenty-four principle character strengths which lead to one of the six higher-level virtues. You can diagnose your strengths and take several other evaluations at the Authentic Happiness Testing Center at the site developed by Seligman, www.authentichappiness.org. Here are the virtues and their attendant strengths:

- WISDOM: curiosity; love of learning; judgment; ingenuity; emotional intelligence; perspective
- COURAGE: valor; perseverance; integrity
- HUMANITY: kindness; loving
- JUSTICE: citizenship; fairness; leadership
- TEMPERANCE: self-control; prudence; humility
- TRANSCENDENCE: appreciation of beauty and excellence; gratitude; hope; spirituality; forgiveness; humor; zest

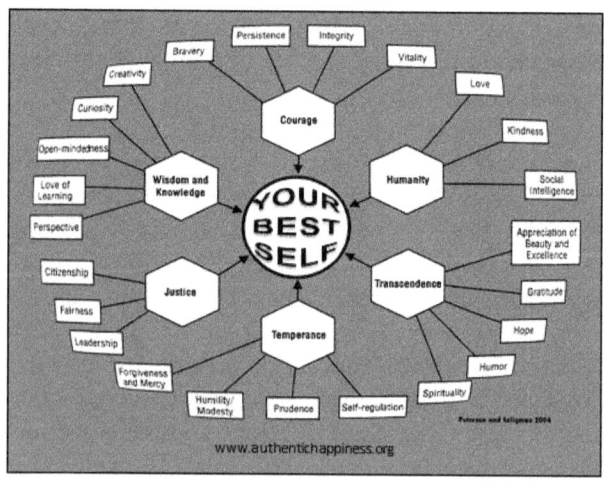

6,000,000 MINUTES ON THE CLOCK

Everyone will have a different opinion on the relative value of each of these strengths, and there is no scale that determines the relative value of each. It is perfectly natural that we will give higher value to those strengths which we possess to a higher degree.

You're probably familiar with some version of the 80/20 principle. In most of our undertakings, including work, 80% of our results come from 20% of our efforts. If you think about the times you've been really productive, on a hot streak, in *flow*, you were accomplishing a lot with relatively little effort. In those situations, you felt great and it was easy to love your work. The other 80% of the time – well, that's another story.

One of the benefits of taking the kinds of evaluations listed above is finding out the 20% that will yield 80%. Some people may see taking such evaluations as a waste of time, but nothing is more wasteful than dedicating 80% of your time and effort for a yield of 20%. That's an outcome/input ratio of 1:4. You would do better to find the time to learn how to reverse that outcome/input ratio from 1:4 to 4:1.

As an example, take the character strengths test. There are 24 character strengths measured in this test. Your top 5 character strengths are the 20% that yield 80% of your results. It's important to know what those strengths are so you can fully utilize them to achieve your goals.

You'll also find out your greatest character weaknesses. We all have some, and it's not a good investment of time and effort to turn those weaknesses into strengths. However, by becoming aware of your greatest weaknesses, you can minimize the damage they might cause you. The weaknesses will likely never help you move forward; your goal is to keep them from moving you backward.

To Thine Own Self Be True

This is eHarmony's Mission Statement:
"To empower people with the knowledge and inspiration needed to grow and strengthen their most important relationships for a lifetime of happiness."

The Compatibility Matching System™ was developed and patented by eHarmony as a scientific approach to matchmaking. The 436-question relationship questionnaire creates a personality profile that describes you in areas like agreeableness, conscientiousness, openness, emotional stability, and extroversion. They also create a compatibility profile, outlining the type of person with whom you are most likely to develop a long-term relationship.

eHarmony's system was developed with personal matchmaking in mind, but its scientific approach to finding one's soul mate was a little out-of-the-box at the time. However, its likelihood of success seems greater than the traditional alternatives. Are you really likely to meet your perfect match just because you happen to work in the same office, live in the same building, or patronize the same bar on the same night?

Whether you're looking for a perfect mate or a perfect career, what you're looking for is compatibility. The most important factor for success in finding a good match is knowing who you are. The purpose of any personality test is not to tell you what you should be doing or who you should love. Its purpose is to give you some additional insight into who *you* are, in all your complex, unique beauty.

Please don't ever start telling yourself that "I should be a (fill-in-the-blank) because my personality test said so." It said no such thing. A personality test *might* indicate that you have certain traits that *might* be helpful in a certain line of work, but that's all.

If you have no clear idea of what you want for a career, and if you need a little guidance on what might be a good fit, a test like Myers-Briggs can be useful. If you think there's a field where you might want to work, but you don't know if it's a good match, taking the test might be a good starting point.

For example, you may have an interest in a sales position because you get to travel and meet people and because the potential money is good. However, your personality test indicates a low threshold for rejection, which might be a problem, as it could cause burnout. The test may also show you have a high level of persistence, which would be an asset in sales. This example illustrates how a personality test can offer guidance, but cannot determine whether you are suited for a job.

It's hard to be good at something that doesn't feel natural. Ultimately, you want to find something that feels like a natural fit, not a square peg in a round hole. It's your best chance for success *and* happiness.

6,000,000 MINUTES ON THE CLOCK

WHAT DRIVES YOU?

My favorite definition of *inspire* is "to breathe life into." This definition has medical connotations, though it transcends the purely medical. This definition also makes it clearer that *inspire* is the opposite of *expire*, which in medical terms means to die. To be inspired, then, is the beginning of life for whatever you're inspired to do. By implication, when you are not inspired to do something, eventually that something will expire. First, we have inspiration; then to keep the spirit alive, we have respiration. Finally, without respiration, we have expiration.

When you are inspired to do something, you are pulled toward it, not pushed toward it. There is an irresistible draw to create something more than currently exists. Could Thomas Edison have created the electric light (not to mention thousands of other inventions) if he were not inspired, drawn irresistibly to create something that would transform mankind as much as any invention in history? Edison could certainly push himself (twenty-hour workdays were not uncommon), but he never felt the push; he only felt the pull, so he rarely tired or thought to give up.

Have you ever noticed that our most noble professions are given a term that is not bestowed on more mundane occupations? That term is *calling*. Calling is most closely associated with religious vocations, but a vocation can be any occupation to which one feels drawn. Most callings and vocations have something in common - their primary purpose is to serve others. Those with a true calling in any profession not only become the most successful in that profession, but they are also sought out above others for their services. You would not seek out a doctor who was in it for the prestige or money. You would not seek out a priest who was in it for the power. You would not seek out a teacher for your child who was in it for the summer vacations. You want to know that the main reason those people are in those professions is because they were called into them by the opportunity to make life better for people like you.

When you're inspired, you have to channel a seemingly endless source of energy. Your body may tire, but your spirit never does. Rather than feeling like a donkey who is being prodded forward with a stick (and maybe a carrot), you feel like a dog who is tugging at the leash to run to the next adventure. To use another analogy, when you are inspired, you may not always know the best way to position the rudder, but your sails are always full.

When you're inspired, your passion burns with the steady intensity of Thomas Edison's successful light bulb. You find yourself thinking of ways to channel that passion to get the most out of it. When you're inspired, your passion becomes more than what you do - it becomes a large part of who you are. It also feels effortless.

Flipping Pyramids

Anyone who has ever taken a psychology course is familiar with Maslow's Hierarchy of Needs. Abraham Maslow developed his theory in 1943. The hierarchy is, in descending order:
- **Self-Actualization** (morality, creativity, spontaneity)

6,000,000 MINUTES ON THE CLOCK

- **Esteem** (achievement, confidence, respect from others)
- **Love/Belonging** (friendship, family, sexual intimacy)
- **Safety** (physical security, employment, health, family)
- **Physiological** (breathing, food, water, sleep, sex)

Maslow theorized that, until one's needs are met at the lower levels, one cannot or will not devote energy to meeting needs at the higher levels. This assumption is valid - you can't focus on your job if you haven't had enough sleep or food; you can't focus on friendships if you are about to lose your job; you can't focus on becoming a more well-rounded person when a loved one is battling a life-threatening disease. The hierarchy of needs is one way of measuring how well we are achieving our full potential.

There is a similar hierarchy when we look at our work. If you are out of work, it can become a desperate struggle just to meet the physiological needs at the bottom of the hierarchy. When you do get a job, you hope it will pay enough to meet your physiological needs. You seek to stay with an employer and hopefully get some raises and promotions in order to fulfill your safety needs. However, when a job is just a job, it won't provide much more than these basic needs. Because these jobs neither demand much nor provide much, you may put your back into it, but not your heart and soul.

Most people aspire to have more than a job - they want a career. A career is a series of jobs that enables you to move up on the hierarchy of needs. (By the way, if you have a career, don't go on about it to people who just have jobs. It annoys them and makes you look like a snob.) A career will usually enable you to buy more of the things that people seek on the lower level of needs.

6,000,000 MINUTES ON THE CLOCK

The most attractive aspect of a career is that it offers the opportunity to fulfill our esteem needs. If we did not consider esteem to be so highly valued, people would not work to earn a Ph.D. in English Literature for the opportunity to teach a core class at the local community college. They would go to a two-year trade school and learn plumbing, where they could then go out and charge $75 an hour for their services.

If you're lucky, a job leads to a career. If you're luckier still, your career becomes your vocation. A vocation is defined as an occupation or profession for which a person is especially suited or qualified. Someone who merely works in a job may be a square peg in a round hole. Someone who builds a career is likely to be a square peg in a square hole, though more careers are made by reshaping a round peg into a square one than by reshaping a square hole into a round one. With a vocation, you are not only a square peg in a square hole; you are the right size peg for that hole.

Finally, we have the pinnacle of the work hierarchy, the calling. We often think of callings in terms of religions, but a calling can be for any work that benefits others primarily and the worker secondarily. A calling is not work that one does for selfish reasons.

6,000,000 MINUTES ON THE CLOCK

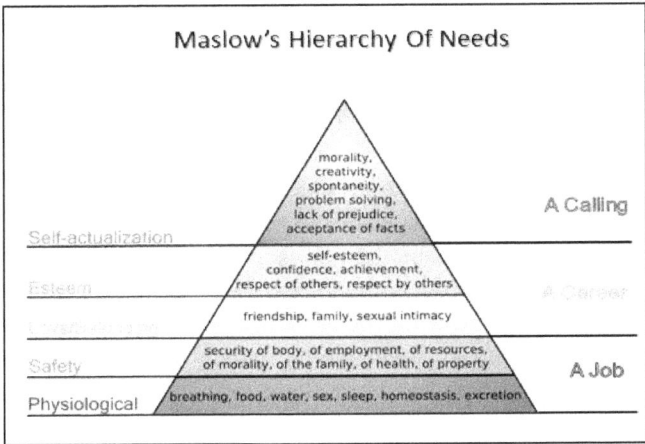

When you merely have a job, you do the job for the pay. If there is any non-monetary benefit to the job, it won't keep you from leaving for a small raise in pay.

With a career, there are benefits beyond pay. You are unlikely to change careers if you could not make as much money in another career, even if you enjoyed the work more.

When you have a vocation, you continuously find it hard to believe that you actually get paid to do something you love. You are not about to give up the financial benefits, but they begin to assume secondary importance to what you receive beyond the paycheck.

Finally, a calling is work that you would pay money to others for the privilege of performing. You are so drawn to do that work, and you are so called by that work that it doesn't matter what you have to do in order to work in that field - you will do it. With a vocation, a person usually starts out with a skill set that makes that vocation a rewarding and easy choice. With a calling, a skill set may have to be acquired through years of training, and even then it might not be enough.

When viewed through the prism of Maslow's Hierarchy of Needs, most jobs take a bottom-up approach. The job promises to provide money in exchange for work, and that money can be used to supply one's basic needs. The reason most people can't get passionate about their jobs is that the job doesn't provide an opportunity to release their passions. Without passion for your work, the most you are likely to become in that work is "competent", which means you are capable of competing (but not necessarily winning).

A calling takes a top-down approach regarding the hierarchy of needs. A calling speaks to something inside the individual that promises to make them a better person, typically by providing the opportunity for that person to make the world a better place. A calling will provide you with the needs at the top of the hierarchy first. The more basic of needs get met as the effect of being passionate about the work leads to being more than competent in performing it. By excellently providing something of value to people, they then provide the means to meet all the basic needs.

Becoming your calling requires a top-down approach to Maslow's Hierarchy of Needs. You begin by realizing that you are not a human being having a spiritual experience; you are a spiritual being having a human experience.

The lower levels focus on feeding the physical needs alone. They can often do that at the expense of the soul and the mind. At the lower levels, there is no feeding of the soul; at most one can hope that the soul isn't being harmed by one's work. This is not to say that there is no value to work that provides only a paycheck. If a certain kind of work did not provide value to others, people would not pay for it, leading to its elimination.

The work you would most want to do, the work that you would do for no pay, the work that never seems like work, that work is your calling. It's possible to transform your current job into your calling, but it's tough working from the bottom up to make such a change. It's also not a good idea to quit your job, pitch a tent in the woods, and contemplate your true calling for the next year.

First look at your current situation and see if there is the potential to transform your job into a calling, to be pulled rather than pushed into getting up each day and going to work. In the meantime, do some soul-searching to ask yourself what kind of work you could do that:

a) would give you a sense of purpose;

b) would be within your capabilities at some point;

c) would enable you to meet your more basic needs as well.

It might take years to find your true calling, but the first step in finding your true calling is to realize you have one and to begin looking for it.

Motivation is Good; Inspiration is Better

People are inspired to greatness; they are almost never motivated to it. Inspiration pulls you; motivation pushes you. It's just too exhausting to be pushed all the way to greatness. If you're merely motivated by family, friends, peers, greed, fear, competitors, enemies, or a thousand other "motivating factors," you may achieve greatness, but it will feel empty and, more importantly, it will be fleeting. Greatness built on motivation without inspiration is like a foundation that is made with concrete that has too much sand and not enough cement. It may look solid, but time quickly exposes the weakness, and whatever was built on that foundation soon collapses.

If you remember reading Mark Twain's *The Adventures of Tom Sawyer* in school, you may recall

6,000,000 MINUTES ON THE CLOCK

Tom using psychology to get his friend Ben to whitewash the fence for him, a task that Tom despised doing. Tom seduced Ben to take over the task by acting as though he loved to whitewash and that he didn't think Ben was capable of doing the job properly:

"He had discovered a great law of human action, without knowing it – namely, that in order to make a man or a boy covet a thing, it is only necessary to make the thing difficult to attain. If he had been a great and wise philosopher, like the writer of this book, he would now have comprehended that Work consists of whatever a body is obliged to do, and that Play consists of whatever a body is not obliged to do."

There is a fundamental reason why money doesn't work as well as a motivator as most people might think. Money doesn't work as a motivator in practice as well as in theory because we tend to think of money as the cause, as the motivator, if you will. **Money isn't the cause; it's the effect.**

It is natural to think that if you are doing something for money, money is the cause of what you are doing. But money is the effect of what you are doing. A cause must first exist in order for you to be motivated by it. Money that you earn from work does not exist until you create it through your work.

When talking about money here, we are referring to the creation of wealth. You create wealth when you work to provide goods and services of value to others. The creation of wealth, as represented by money, is the effect of your work. At most, money as a motivator provides the opportunity to create wealth.

6,000,000 MINUTES ON THE CLOCK

Frederick Herzberg was an American psychologist who greatly influenced business management with what is generally referred to as the Two-Factor Theory. Herzberg's theory states that people are not content with satisfaction at the lower levels of Maslow's hierarchy of needs. Individuals will also seek gratification of higher-level psychological needs related to achievement, recognition, responsibility, advancement, and the nature of the work itself.

Two-factor theory distinguishes between:
- **Motivators** (challenging work, recognition, responsibility, achievement) that give positive satisfaction arising from intrinsic conditions of the work itself and
- **Hygiene factors** (status, job security, salary, fringe benefits, work conditions) that do not give positive satisfaction, though their absence results in dissatisfaction. These factors are extrinsic to the work itself.

Essentially, **hygiene factors are necessary to prevent an employee from becoming dissatisfied. Motivation factors are needed to motivate an employee to higher performance.** Herzberg further classified workers' actions and how and why they do them. If you perform a work-related action because you *have* to, then that is classed as movement; if you perform a work-related action because you *want* to, then that is classed as motivation.

At some time in his youth, Frederick Herzberg probably read *The Adventures of Tom Sawyer*. Herzberg made a career and influenced business management practices by quantitatively proving what Mark Twain said - work consists of what you have to do and play consists of what you want to do.

What is the environment where you work? If the hygiene factors are lacking or inadequate, it can be hard for you to feel anything but dissatisfied. In such an environment, morale is low, turnover is high, and businesses that don't provide a minimum level of hygiene factors don't stay in business for long.

When a business is just starting up, the environment may be one where the hygiene factors are low, but the motivators are high. Hygiene factors are low because money is tight in most start-ups. The company can't offer security yet, but what they can offer is plenty of opportunity. It can be an exciting environment where everyone is excited about the prospect of building something from scratch as a team. That enthusiasm and dedication should translate into profits at some point. At that point, the employer needs to raise the hygiene factors to an acceptable level.

Old school business thinking was that as long as the business took care of the hygiene factors, it was up to the employees to find their own motivation. If management focused more on people than numbers, an unproductive environment could result. The main reason people stay in such jobs is that the hygiene factors there are better than the hygiene factors elsewhere. People get used to a certain level of salaries and benefits, and they are reluctant to give some of that up for intangibles like recognition and achievement.

The goal is a work environment that offers both the requisite level of hygiene factors and as many motivators as possible. What many business managers fail to recognize is that the way to get workers to be their most productive is to pay them enough that money is not an issue (which does not mean paying them more than anyone else or paying the employee as much as they demand) and then to provide as many motivators as possible.

To help get the proper perspective of money as a motivator, consider this situation. At your place of employment, you feel you are well-paid for the work you do. However, you just found out that two of your co-workers, neither of whom is more productive than you, both earn more than you. Would that news make you suddenly dissatisfied with your level of pay? What if you found out that those two co-workers were more satisfied with their jobs than you? Would you care? That bit of information would be unlikely to raise your level of dissatisfaction.

The situation just described illustrates a point - the best motivators are the ones that have no limits. When someone finds out that co-workers are paid more, they become dissatisfied because they believe that others' higher income must come at their own expense. When someone finds out that co-workers are more satisfied in their jobs, they do not become dissatisfied because satisfaction is not a finite resource. Satisfaction can be created in infinite quantities by those who will benefit most from its creation.

It is unlikely that a worker who found out that others were earning more would go to those co-workers and find out their secret of earning more in order to copy their practices and earn more, too. However, it is at least plausible that someone might approach co-workers who seem more satisfied, to find out their secrets, in the hopes of reaping greater satisfaction on the job, too.

We think of hygiene factors as motivators in part because of the Industrial Revolution. Before the

6,000,000 MINUTES ON THE CLOCK

Industrial Revolution, work was arduous and often dangerous, but for the most part it wasn't routine. Two-thirds of the population worked in agriculture prior to the Industrial Revolution. That work had many drawbacks, but at least there was a certain variety to it.

Prior to the Industrial Revolution, there were no assembly lines. With the advent of the modern factory, tasks were broken down to their smallest elements, and workers would perform those smallest elements continuously.

If you worked at a Ford assembly plant in 1920, you could take pride that you were part of the team that built the Model T, the car that put America on wheels. However, your workday consisted of attaching the front bumper on the driver's side as each car came down the line. Your work involved six separate steps and had to be completed in 42 seconds because that was the pace of the moving assembly line. By the end of the year, you would have attached 171,428 bumpers to 171,428 Model T's. Work like that required a lot of outside direction and supervision. No one can stay self-motivated performing the same routine 86 times an hour, 8 hours a day, 250 days a year.

Non-routine jobs are far more common today. The pace of change requires that jobs evolve continuously to keep up with new technologies and competition. The push for productivity now has workers multi-tasking, as opposed to breaking work down into smaller and smaller increments. The variety of activities in the average workday today makes it easier for workers to maintain interest in their work. The number of workers putting in 10 and 12 hour workdays may be the result of the push for more productivity, but they could not be productive for 10 or 12 hours a day unless the work was able to hold their interest for that long a period.

One of the great motivators is autonomy. We all want to think we are the ones who decide what we are going to do. If you are a parent, you have probably used an If-Then scenario with your child at some time. They can be stated positively or negatively, as a carrot or a stick: "If you clean your room, we can go get ice cream. If you don't clean your room, you can't play any video games." If-Then rewards, and especially punishments, are perceived as reducing one's autonomy.

Autonomy is one of those intrinsic motivators. Intrinsic motivators are delicate things. They can be damaged by, of all things, extrinsic rewards. Bobby Jones was one of the greatest golfers of all time, winning thirteen major tournaments. He also co-founded Augusta National and the Masters Tournament. He was a lawyer by profession and only played golf as an amateur. When asked why he never turned pro, he replied, "When you play for money, it's not love anymore." The lesson of Bobby Jones is: **when people are doing something because of intrinsic motivators, don't muck it up by offering extrinsic rewards.** You will only hurt their performance.

Extrinsic rewards, like money, can send two seemingly contradictory signals at the same time. The first signal is that the task you are performing is valuable and that someone wants to demonstrate appreciation of you performing it with financial compensation. The second signal is that the task you are performing is inherently undesirable and that the only way to entice you to perform this undesirable task is to offer you financial compensation. We prefer the first signal simply because there is an intrinsic element to it: the recognition and appreciation of our performing a task well.

Extrinsic rewards, like money, tend to have a more addictive quality, compared to intrinsic rewards. We easily get used to whatever level of material comfort we currently enjoy, a trait known as adaptation.

We are capable of adapting to the change for the worse, but we certainly don't like it; furthermore, it clouds our attitude toward our work. Also, once we get paid for doing something, it's unlikely we will ever be willing to do it again for free. In such a case, we are willing to give up the good vibes of doing something for the joy of it if we are no longer getting paid to do it. It feels as if we are giving away something of value to someone who should be paying for it.

In order to feel motivated, we need to feel that the work we are performing has some importance, and we also need to feel a certain sense of urgency about it. A sense of urgency and importance isn't hard to come by if you're the attending physician in a hospital emergency room. It may be harder to generate those feelings when you're reviewing expense reports at your company.

There's a reason why every task at work needs to be done. If you don't see how your task fits into the big picture at work, you owe it to yourself to find out how the work you do makes a positive difference in people's lives. Your boss, if he/she is worthy of the position, knows you deserve such knowledge and that such knowledge can be a great motivator.

Your boss should also recognize that once you feel a sense of urgency and importance to your work, the best thing to do is free you to get the work done in the best way you see fit. If you are properly motivated about the purpose of your work, you are also properly motivated to do that work to the best of your ability and as efficiently as possible.

Master of Your Domain

Self-determination theory (SDT) is a theory of motivation developed by Edward L. Deci and Richard M. Ryan at the University of Rochester in the 1980's. SDT contends that humans have three innate psychological needs - competence, autonomy, and relatedness. The three needs cited in SDT can be defined as follows:
- **Competence**: to seek to control the outcome and experience mastery of a task
- **Autonomy**: the universal urge to be the causal agent of one's own life and to act in harmony with one's integrated self, though this action does not mean to be independent of others
- **Relatedness**: the universal desire to interact, be connected to, and experience caring for others

From the Self-Determination Theory web site:

"Within SDT, the nutriments for healthy development and functioning are specified using the concept of basic psychological needs for autonomy, competence, and relatedness. ***To the extent that the needs are ongoingly satisfied, people will develop and function effectively and experience wellness, but to the extent that they are thwarted, people more likely evidence ill-being and non-optimal functioning.*** *The darker sides of human behavior and experience, such as certain types of psychopathology, prejudice, and aggression are*

6,000,000 MINUTES ON THE CLOCK

understood in terms of reactions to basic needs having been thwarted, either developmentally or proximally." (emphasis mine)

Deci and Ryan's studies quantified that people who have their intrinsic needs met on the job are both healthier and, just as important, perform better over time, leading to higher compensation and more wealth. Those who focused on extrinsic rewards, especially money alone, felt more stress, felt less fulfillment and, in the long run, had less success and earned less than their counterparts who focused on intrinsic rewards and let the money take care of itself. Deci and Ryan and others who have followed have shown conclusively that **when you recognize that money is not the cause, but the effect, you end up with more money, and you are far happier on the way to attaining it.**

6,000,000 MINUTES ON THE CLOCK

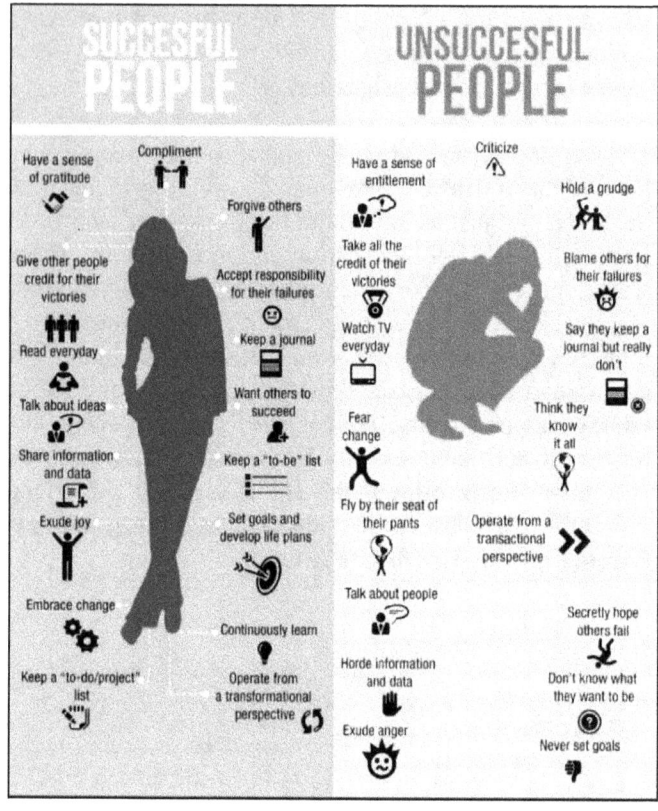

More and more people are pursuing Master's degrees these days. Some are in programs because the job market isn't good for them. Some know they need more than a Bachelor's degree to be competitive in their field. Almost all of them seek what is implied by the title of the degree - they seek mastery of a subject.

As we have become more and more specialized in our jobs, mastery of the skills needed to perform our jobs has become more and more critical to our success. To be a jack of all trades is to be, by default in this era, a master of none. All trades require a level of mastery that makes it almost impossible for the average person to excel in more than a few areas.

We instinctively want to become highly skilled in a field for two important reasons. First, higher skill levels lead to higher compensation - ask any professional athlete. Second - and this reason is more important for most people - mastery leads to greater autonomy. **Mastery of your work skills leads to mastery of your life.**

When a job challenges us beyond our skill levels, we feel stressed. When a job doesn't challenge us at all, we become bored and disengaged. When we are challenged enough that we are fully engaged without being stressed, we are said to be in flow, or in sports parlance, in the zone. There is a sweet spot each of us has where we are energized by the challenge of our work, instead of being either debilitated or disinterested by it.

Because we have a tendency to get bored easily, mastery becomes a moving target. The rapid pace of change necessitates that we all continually upgrade our skills to remain competitive in the workforce. However, this rapid pace of change creates an externally imposed mandate to upgrade one's skills, which we are learning is a poor way to motivate people. We also have an intrinsic desire to upgrade our skills, in part because we don't want to become complacent and bored in our work. But mastery also feels good, and continuous improvement is the best way to maintain that good feeling.

It is never necessary to *be the best*; it is only necessary to *do your best*. When you do your best, you will occasionally be the best, too. Being the best is another one of those extrinsic factors - you are basing your mastery on a comparison to others. Because you can't control the skills and talents of others, you end up ceding your happiness and sense of worth to something beyond your control. Doing your best puts all the control with you, where it belongs. You set the standard; you do the evaluating; you hand out the rewards. And true mastery involves a commitment that, however good you are at something today, your goal is to be a little better tomorrow.

Motivation is more like respiration than inspiration. Motivation doesn't get us breathing, but it can help keep us breathing when breathing gets difficult.

Even when you're inspired, you still need motivation. Inspiration helps you produce a strategy; motivation helps you develop tactics. The best way to get and stay motivated is to find a cause that is bigger than just you.

We generally work harder to prevent disappointing others than to prevent disappointing ourselves. Look for intrinsic reasons to do something. Make the effort because it affects you in positive, intangible ways; not because others think you should do it or because someone or something is prodding you with carrots and sticks.

Finally, make sure you answer the why question before you worry about answering who-what-when-where-how questions. **The proper answer to the why question will provide inspiration *and* keep you motivated.** When you properly answer the why question, you will also find a lot of who-what-when-where-how questions begin to answer themselves.

6,000,000 MINUTES ON THE CLOCK

Getting Along

Animals with bigger brains have more complex social networks, and we humans are at the top of that list. We have large frontal lobes because we have the largest social groups. We have the largest social groups because we could not survive without them.

When you look at humans as a species, it's obvious we did not become the dominant species on the planet because of any purely physical superiority. The only way we survived as a species, much less came to dominate, was because of our ability to develop and maintain complex social networks. What has worked for us as a species for thousands of years also applies to us as individuals. The better we are at developing connections with other people, the better our chances for survival, success, and ultimately, happiness.

Social networks are excellent at offering support when we need it. They are also excellent at providing constraints when we need those, too. There are the obvious examples, such as judicial systems that discourage criminal behavior that is detrimental to the group. There are also the less obvious examples, like posting your activities on Facebook, Youtube, etc.

Before engaging in activity that might be, at a minimum, embarrassing, we now think about the repercussions, should that activity end up on some social networking site. These same social networks help us stay on task when we make a commitment to positive change. If you tell all your friends on social media that you are going to lose ten pounds in the next two months, you know you will have to provide an accounting to them at the end of the period.

6,000,000 MINUTES ON THE CLOCK

The best relationships are built on five attributes: respect, shared experience, mutual enjoyment of each other's company, trust, and reciprocity. The ability to establish and maintain all five of these attributes in a relationship is one reason why the number of meaningful relationships we can handle is limited. The importance of a relationship in our lives is also based largely on to what degree these five attributes are present.

When we are free to choose a relationship, the ability to respect someone is one of the first requirements. If we don't respect someone, it's unlikely we will want to establish any kind of relationship. Some relationships that are established for us, such as with our parents, assume a level of respect. Once we have the option of discontinuing such a relationship, the respect must be earned. The loss of respect for a person can be an instant relationship killer, such as when we discover a friend has been cheating on a spouse or a business partner.

Shared experiences bond people together, especially if the experience is profoundly positive or negative. A profoundly positive experience is something on the order of bringing a child into the world together, not merely taking a cruise together. Experiences that involved hardship, danger, or suffering are often the catalyst for our deepest friendships. Many a lifelong friend has been made on the battlefield. Misery truly does love company.

We want to have relationships when we enjoy spending time with someone. However, we have to spend a lot of time with people whose company we don't particularly enjoy. Such situations are especially true at work, where we don't get to choose our co-workers. The people we want to spend time with are those who share some of our interests and who also possess enough social skills to make their presence something to be enjoyed, rather than merely tolerated.

Along with respect, trust must be present at the beginning of a relationship, or it is unlikely to form. Trust is greatest where the relationship is deepest. If a casual friend failed to keep a piece of shared gossip secret, the relationship would lose value, even though we might not feel compelled to end the relationship. On the other hand, if we found out our spouse had been unfaithful, a betrayal of trust on that level by someone that close is almost certain to irreparably damage the relationship.

Even in the strongest, most enduring, and most noble of relationships, certain rules, mostly unspoken, still apply. In order to maintain the relationship and reap its benefits, it is necessary to abide by these codes.

As a social construct, *reciprocity* means that in response to friendly actions, people are frequently much nicer and much more cooperative than what could be expected by the self-interest model; conversely, in response to hostile actions, reciprocity is frequently much nastier and sometimes quite brutal. Reciprocity encompasses the concepts of the Golden Rule, mutual back scratching, quid pro quo, and an eye for an eye.

Reciprocity is not the same as altruism or even gift giving. Altruism is helping those less fortunate, with the only reward being the positive feelings that result from the good deed. Gift giving is not typically based on need, but rather on the desire to make someone else happy. When a grandparent gives a gift to a grandchild, neither altruism nor reciprocity is a factor in that action.

Reciprocity is based both on the other party's intentions as well as the consequences of their actions. We actually feel a greater obligation to reciprocate when someone attempts to do us a favor that doesn't work out than we do for someone who inadvertently benefits us. Reciprocity is based on a trading of favors, as opposed to a formal negotiation or contract.

In addition to positive reciprocity, there is also negative reciprocity, which might be construed as retaliation or revenge. Negative reciprocity, unlike positive reciprocity, doesn't have the expectation of gain. Other than the pleasure of getting back at someone who has harmed you, the only other benefit to negative reciprocity may be to discourage such acts by the perpetrator or others in the future. In certain circles, such as the Mafia, to not retaliate when you've been wronged is taken as a sign of weakness and invites even worse abuses in the future.

Our instinct for reciprocity is so strong that a person will feel obligated to return a favor, even if the favor was unrequested, as was demonstrated in an experiment by Dennis Regan in 1971. Regan led subjects to believe they were in an art appreciation experiment with a partner, who was really Regan's assistant. In the experiment, the assistant would disappear briefly and bring back a soft drink for the subject. After the art experiment was through, the assistant asked the subject to buy a raffle ticket. In the control group the assistant behaved in exactly the same manner, but did not buy the subject a drink. The subjects who had received the favor, a soft drink, bought more raffle tickets than those in the control group, despite the fact that they had not solicited the drink or any favor from the assistant. Surveys completed by the subjects after they finished the experiment showed that whether they personally liked the assistant or not had no effect on how many tickets they bought.

6,000,000 MINUTES ON THE CLOCK

One problem of reciprocity focuses on the unequal profit obtained from the concept of reciprocal concessions. The emotional burden to repay bothers some more than others, causing some to overcompensate with more than what was given originally. In the Regan study, subjects paid more money for the tickets than the cost of the unrequested soft drink. Whether it's unsolicited address stickers in the mail from some charity or flowers passed out by a religious cult at the airport, people who want something from us know that the best way to get it is to give us something that is unsolicited (and of lower value) first, and then wait for the reciprocity gene to kick in before making their sales pitch. Without our instinct for reciprocity, free samples might cease to exist.

In this world, we have *social norms* and *market norms*. Social norms involve the interactions between humans. They are about helping each other and getting along. They are the glue that holds a society together. They are biological. Market norms involve a bottom line. They are transaction-based. They can be precisely measured. They are mechanical.

We are all familiar with the old saying, "It's a pleasure doing business with you." Conducting business with people should be a pleasurable experience, but there should be clear boundaries where social norms rule and where market norms rule. In any business situation, there is a potential clash of social norms and market norms, and any attempt to mix the two can lead to real problems.

The first thing to realize is that **when social norms collide with market norms, social norms lose.** This collision almost always occurs when market norms invade the world of social norms. For example, many budding romantic relationships have come to a screeching halt because, at some point, the guy brought up how much he had spent on dates and that he wasn't getting anything in return. That one comment shifted the relationship from social norms to market norms.

In business relationships, market norms should rule. Certainly, every business should treat their customers and their employees with respect. But the business will have neither customers nor employees unless it maintains an acceptable bottom line. In the long term, all employees must be judged on their ability to add value to the business. All customers must be judged on whether they add to or subtract from the bottom line.

If you are an employee, the relationship with your employer should be based first on a fair exchange of labor for money. That said, social norms are one of the best ways to engender employee loyalty. We may stay because we need the paycheck, but we want to stay when we feel appreciated, which is a large purpose of social norms. You remember when an employer says "thank you" when distributing paychecks. Little things make a big difference.

In social relationships, social norms should rule. When you are invited to a friend's house for dinner, you bring a nice bottle of wine as a gift; you don't offer to "pay the tab" at the end of the evening. When your neighbor asks to borrow your lawn mower, you lend it with the expectation he will return the favor in the future (reciprocity); you don't charge him rent.

Social norms should always prevail when a higher calling is involved. People are more inclined to donate blood when cookies and juice are offered as a thank you than when cash is offered as compensation. If people want to do something for altruistic reasons, you will offend them and prompt them to withdraw support if you bring money into the equation. The good feeling we get when we do something to help others is priceless, so the worst thing one can do is attempt to put a price on it.

If you introduce market norms where social norms prevail, market norms will almost always win. But know that social norms may never return and that they never forget, either.

When someone makes a mistake with market norms, the typical result is a loss of business, but nothing more. People who are consistently bad with market norms may end up going out of business, but they probably won't become social pariahs.

Making mistakes with social norms can be far more costly. Our social network, our relationship support system, is undergirded by social norms. When we are clumsy with social norms, or when we attempt to replace social norms with market norms, we risk knocking that entire support system out from under us.

Not only do we risk relationship penalties from misuse of social norms, misuse of social norms can have a more devastating effect on our finances than misuse of market norms. You have to make a living from your friends because your enemies won't do business with you. Poor use of social norms can turn friends into enemies, with the result that you have no friends and no customers.

Social media has been called many things, but a couple of the more accurate descriptions are word of mouth on digital steroids and the world's largest referral program in history. Social media has become the most importance place for a business to be if they intend to stay in business. While it may be called social media, it is actually driven by market norms.

6,000,000 MINUTES ON THE CLOCK

While keeping in touch with others' activities is a major driver of social media, the real reason for the popularity of social media is the almost endless opportunities for self-promotion. The whole purpose of LinkedIn is to enable people to promote themselves in the business environment. Twitter and Facebook enable us to promote ourselves both professionally and personally.

Over time, our social media postings paint a picture of us to others. We may not be aware of how often we may post on a particular topic, but we are keenly aware of Facebook friends who are obsessed with their pets, grandchildren, politics, or what they are having for lunch. These constant postings offer the opportunity for many people to get to know you better. Whether or not that's a good thing depends on what you're posting.

One of the more troubling trends with social media involves generations Y and Z, the young people who use social media in greater proportion for their socializing than older people. They may be more adept at communicating in a digital world, but for those relationships to have any real-world value, they must eventually take place in the real world, which means face-to-face. While social media may enable people, especially younger ones, to speak up in situations where they might remain silent in person (not necessarily a bad thing, either), the reliance on social media also seems to be hampering the ability to write and speak effectively in more traditional settings.

Goal(s)!

Since it was first published in 1989, Steven Covey's book *The 7 Habits of Highly Effective People* has sold more than 25 million copies worldwide. It ranks in the top ten best-selling non-fiction books of all time. Habit 2 is titled "Begin with the End in Mind." The author explains:

"To begin with the end in mind means to start with a clear understanding of your destination. It means to know where you're going so that you better understand where you are now and so that the steps you take are always in the right direction… we may be very busy, we may be very efficient, but we will also be truly <u>effective</u> only when we begin with the end in mind."

Becoming inspired and motivated is like building the powertrain to the vehicle that will enable you to become successful and happy. The setting of goals is like building the steering and GPS systems that help steer you to your destination. Put in more primitive terms, **inspiration and motivation are your sails; goals are your rudder.**

Before you can set goals, you must first determine what your mission is. When you think of your mission, you should think in terms of a personal philosophy and set of values that don't change. Goals can and should change as needed. Goals adjust to the outer world and your inner changes; moreover, changing goals as needed enables you to stay true to your mission.

In recent years, American business has embraced the concept of SMART goals. The acronym stands for **S**pecific, **M**easurable, **A**chievable, **R**ealistic, and **T**ime-targeted. The concept of SMART goals contends that goals that are difficult to achieve and specific tend to increase performance more than goals that are not.

6,000,000 MINUTES ON THE CLOCK

Setting SMART goals affects outcomes in four ways:
- **Choice**: goals narrow attention and direct efforts to goal-relevant activities and away from counter-productive or irrelevant activities.
- **Effort**: goals can lead to more effort, especially because a goal almost always exceeds the current level of performance.
- **Persistence**: Someone becomes more prone to work through the inevitable setbacks if pursuing a goal.
- **Cognition**: Goals can lead individuals to develop and change their behavior in the long run, even after goals are met.

Because SMART goals are specific, they avoid some of the biggest flaws in goal-setting - irrelevance and ambiguity. SMART goals can be very effective, but only if the goals themselves are worthwhile. Before goals, especially SMART goals, are created and implemented, everyone who is expected to meet those goals needs to believe that what they are working toward is worth the effort to get there. SMART goals presume a commitment; they don't create it.

The need to buy into a goal before attempting to achieve it is the reason for inspiration and motivation first. If you are setting goals only for yourself, becoming inspired and motivated can be fairly easy. If you have to inspire and motivate others, that's defined as Leadership. Leadership is in essence inspiring and motivating others to do what they would not do on their own. For our purposes, we will limit our discussion to personal goal-setting. If you are able to achieve your own goals, that's enough for now. Besides, you can't lead others to achieve goals if you're incapable of achieving your own goals.

6,000,000 MINUTES ON THE CLOCK

SMART goals are most effective in steady-state situations, rather than ones that require major changes. SMART goals tend to focus on effects more than causes. They measures effects more than attempt to change behaviors. Since major outcome changes almost always require major behavioral changes first, setting up behavioral goals is a necessary prerequisite to setting up SMART goals.

You may think that setting small goals leads to less success because you aren't pushing yourself, but that isn't the case. **Small goals that get accomplished do more to spur us on than do large single goals that always seem to be over the horizon.** The positive reinforcement that achieving small goals provides enables us to continue making progress toward larger goals.

Research shows that small goals, known in psychology as proximal goals, have more effect than large goals, known as distal goals. In one study, elementary school students who did poorly in math were broken into two groups. One group was given the distal goal of completing seven thirty-minute math modules by the end of the seventh session. The other group was given the proximal goal of completing one module during each session. Both groups were functioning at the same math skills level at the beginning. On the final test, the distal goals group solved 45% of the problems; the proximal goals group solved 81%. The only difference in the two groups in this study was in the way the goals were presented. The distal group was thinking like a python, trying to swallow the problem whole; the proximal group was thinking like a piranha, biting the problem into small chunks. The results speak for themselves.

6,000,000 MINUTES ON THE CLOCK

"So, what are we aiming for, Timmy – The Nobel Prize or 'Inspected by No. 7'?"

Dean Karlan is an economics professor at Yale University. Along with colleagues Barry Nalebuff and Ian Ayres, he developed stickK.com. StickK.com offers you the opportunity, through "Commitment Contracts," to show to yourself and others the value you put on achieving your goals.

The four steps involved on stickK.com are:

1. **Select your goal.** Your goal can be anything you want. No guidance is offered on setting appropriate or attainable goals.
2. **Set the stakes.** You have the option of putting money on the line. If you don't succeed in meeting your goal, stickK will send your money to one of three options - a friend, a charity, or an "anti-charity," which is an organization you choose that is against what you stand for. The thought of

financially supporting the other side can be a powerful motivator.
3. **Get a referee.** Invite someone trustworthy to be your referee and report to stickK.com your success or failure.
4. **Add friends for support.** Your friends can supply support, peer pressure, or whatever you might need to help you meet your goal.

A study done in Scotland in 1992 demonstrated the healing power of written goals. A group of sixty patients who had hip or knee replacement surgery were studied during rehab. Movement is very painful after such surgery, but it is essential to get moving as soon as possible. Blood clots can form, and scar tissue can form in the joints, destroying flexibility.

Each patient received a booklet with his/her rehab schedule. In the back of the booklet were several additional blank pages with a heading: "My goals for this week are____:" The patients were asked to write down their personal rehab goals for each week, such as when and how far they planned to walk that week.

When the researchers followed up with the patients three months later, they found a profound difference between those who had written down weekly goals and those who hadn't. The patients who had written goals had begun walking nearly twice as fast as the ones who hadn't. They became mobile almost three times faster.

Many of the plans focused on how the patient would deal with pain or some other setback. These patients recognized that there would be times when meeting their goals would become especially difficult, so they dealt with the temptation to quit by having an action plan to get them past their worst moments.

6,000,000 MINUTES ON THE CLOCK

Almost everyone responds better to positive reinforcement than the negative kind. For that reason, goals are more effective when stated in positive terms rather than negative ones. A goal that is stated in terms of what someone is moving toward, rather than what they hope to leave behind, will be more effective. For example, it's preferable to state a goal of becoming sober, as opposed to stating it as stopping drinking.

Writing down goals has been proven to increase the chances for success. Writing down goals creates a greater sense of clarity and commitment. However, clarity depends on how the goal is actually stated.

Most goals are so vaguely stated that it can be impossible to judge whether someone has succeeded or failed. Some of the goals people have made on stickK.com include "lose weight," "drink less," "start approaching attractive women," "eat/live clean," and "do whatever I want." These goals leave so much wiggle room that it can be easy for the individual to claim success. Any progress is to be encouraged, but progress isn't the same thing as victory.

Goals need to be quantifiable, which means that, whenever possible, a date and an amount of some kind should be part of a goal. The vaguely stated goals in the previous paragraph don't have any numbers attached to them, so it is difficult to measure progress, success, or failure. A referee for one of these people should insist that they come up with an amount and a date before agreeing to help.

For the person who wants to lose weight, referees should know how much weight and by what date. To aid progress, they should get a timetable of incremental weight losses and dates. Recall the elementary school math students who had their goals broken into seven individual modules, and they performed much better as a result. If an overall goal were to lose 30 pounds in 300 days, target dates for losing 5, 10, 15, 20, and 25 pounds should also be set. These sub-goals provide ongoing incentives while reducing procrastination. Missing a sub-goal should not be considered a failure, but rather a reminder that additional effort might be needed to reach the overall goal.

Very often we underestimate our own abilities. As a result, we set goals that are too modest. Goals should have a lot of flexibility to be adjusted upward and a lot less flexibility to be adjusted downward. The ability to adjust goals upward easily enables progress to occur as fast as possible. The ability to adjust goals downward uneasily reduces the tendency to want to backslide at the first sign of difficulty; but having the flexibility to adjust downward can also prevent complete abandonment of a goal. Even if a goal has to be adjusted downward, there is likely still an element of progress already, which should not go unclaimed.

If you have first discovered your inspiration, your motivation, and your mission before you start setting goals, then you should not have any goals that conflict with your personal values. Such goals are unlikely to be achieved, and even if they were, it would be a hollow victory.

In addition to not conflicting with personal values, goals should not conflict with each other. One way of avoiding conflicting goals is to have a clear priority of goals. A first priority might be to reduce spending and increase savings. There might also be a goal of exercising more and losing weight. Both of those goals can be worked on simultaneously. However, joining a health club to promote more exercise may increase spending and reduce saving, which is in clear conflict with your first priority goal.

Psychologists Robert Emmons and Laura King have demonstrated in a series of studies that conflicting goals create three main problems:
- **Worry** - The effort to reconcile competing or conflicting demands creates stress.
- **Lower productivity** - Conflict leads to confusion, which leads to paralysis, or at least inefficiency.
- **Physical and mental health problems** - Greater anxiety and depression are most common emotional problems, which lead to poorer health overall.

If you hate having unfinished business, you probably don't procrastinate. The reason you hate unfinished business is the Zeigarnik effect, named after Russian psychologist Bluma Zeigarnik. Her studies demonstrated that unfinished business preys on our minds, while completing a task allows us to forget about it and move on.

When we have an uncompleted task or an unreached goal, it's like the seven-note musical riff commonly known as "shave-and-a-haircut…two-bits." (You might recognize it as the banjo riff from *The Beverly Hillbillies,* right before a commercial break.) Many a laugh has been induced where the last two notes are held in abeyance for what is only seconds, but seems like an eternity. Until we hear the last two notes, we can't move on.

Follow up studies have revealed another aspect of the Zeigarnik effect. When we have an unfinished task or unaccomplished goal, we can alleviate the distraction of it by making a written plan to complete the task or accomplish the goal. Once a plan is in place, our unconscious mind stops nagging our conscious mind and reverts to simple reminders to accomplish what has been promised.

Whenever we can take action that will help us achieve multiple goals simultaneously, it makes sense to do so. If dining out less often and eating at home will increase your savings and reduce your waistline at the same time, that's a double incentive to whip up something in the kitchen instead of making reservations. Viewed from another perspective, frequent dining out can reduce your wallet while expanding the butt that sits upon it.

Finally, every accomplished goal deserves a reward for reaching it. The reward should be proportionate with the difficulty of reaching that particular goal. Losing five pounds does not merit a new car, nor does losing one hundred pounds merit a mere bouquet of flowers. If a goal is worthwhile, the change resulting from its accomplishment will be rewarding. The act of accomplishment will also be rewarding. The additional reward is the motivation to keep going during the task of reaching the goal. During that time, when the hard work is being done but the rewards are not yet forthcoming, we need all the help we can get to keep us moving forward.

For most of us, peer pressure is most overwhelming in adolescence, but it is prevalent throughout our lives, in every group. Peer pressure is normally thought of in negative terms, and with good cause, especially when we think of teenagers doing reckless things because their peers goaded them into doing it. The parents of those teens might also be giving in to peer pressure. They might not be smoking pot or smashing mailboxes, but they might be going deeply into debt trying to maintain the lifestyle of their peer group.

Because the people with whom we associate can have a huge influence on our behavior, it's important to look at how they might be influencing the habits we develop. If our associates or co-workers have bad habits, there's a good chance we will develop some of those same habits. In general, if you hang around with people who behave better than you do, you will begin to behave better. The opposite, of course, is also true. Peer pressure exists, even when it isn't obvious.

Finding just one person who lives the way you want to live can be the turning point. In fact, far more people make major changes for the better because of a single person, not a single event. That single person might be a love interest, although those situations leading to long-term success are rarer than the romantic in us would like to believe. More often, the agent of change is a friend or colleague who is a positive role model, who supports your desire for change, and who introduces you to other people who can also serve as role models. Because these people believe in you, you begin to believe in yourself, and you begin to believe that you can become better.

80/20

It's unlikely you've ever heard of Vilfredo Pareto (1848-1923). He was an Italian engineer, sociologist, economist, political scientist, and philosopher. His greatest contribution is probably the theory that bears his name, the Pareto Principle. The reason you probably don't know of Pareto or his principle is because the more common name for the Pareto Principle is the 80/20 Rule.

6,000,000 MINUTES ON THE CLOCK

Pareto developed his principle by making such diverse observations as 80% of the land in Italy was owned by 20% of the population, and 20% of the pea pods in his garden contained 80% of the peas. Across the spectrum of human endeavors, there is a consistent pattern that **20% of the input is responsible for 80% of the output.**

The 80/20 Rule is so important because, like many of the keys to success, it is counter-intuitive. We tend to think that equal inputs should have equal outputs. When identical efforts do not yield identical results, there is an unfairness to the system that must be rectified. Instead of focusing our efforts on the productive 20%, we spend too much time and effort in an almost always futile effort to lift the bottom 80% to the level of the top 20%. When the two groups do reach some level of parity, it is almost always the result of the top 20% being pulled down, rather than any success in lifting the bottom 80% up.

Joseph M. Juran was born in Romania in 1904. He emigrated to the U.S. in 1912, and his family settled in Minnesota. After graduating from college, Juran became an engineer at Western Electric. In 1941, Juran stumbled across the works of Pareto, resulting in a major shift in world economic power.

Expanding upon Pareto's principle, Juran developed a method of quality management that centered on the theory that 80% of quality problems are caused by 20% of the causes. Juran also argued that human problems - mainly a resistance to change - were at the core of most quality problems. Juran was also one of the first to recognize and analyze the cost of poor quality.

In the early 1950's, American industries weren't interested in Juran's theories. They were the world leaders, and there was a resistance to change. Japan was another story. They were rebuilding an economic base after the devastation of World War II. Japanese products at that time had a reputation for poor quality. In the 1950's and well into the 1960's, "made in Japan" was synonymous with "junk".

Juran became a guru to Japanese management. By the early 1970's, the quality of Japanese products was equal to or better than the competition from the rest of the world. At that time, all anyone had to do was drive a Toyota Corolla and a Ford Pinto back-to-back to see the genius of Joseph Juran. American business finally embraced Juran and his theories when ignoring them was no longer an option. Just as it took the Japanese nearly two decades to reap the rewards of Juran's theories of quality improvement, American businesses would spend the better part of two decades being uncompetitive before the quality gap narrowed appreciably.

If we know from Pareto that 20% of inputs create 80% of outputs, and if we know from Juran that 80% of problems are caused by 20% of causes, we also know that we can greatly improve who we are by focusing on these two areas.

We all have certain strengths that have served us well throughout our lives. These strengths probably came naturally to us. We tend to take them for granted, which is another way of saying we undervalue them. Also, we all have some glaring weaknesses that tend to erase much of the progress that our strengths could be providing to us.

To become as efficient as you can become, your efforts should be focused as follows:

6,000,000 MINUTES ON THE CLOCK

1. Recognize, develop, and utilize your strengths to their fullest advantage. "Lead with your strength" is not just some slogan; it is practical advice.
2. Recognize your most glaring weaknesses and then work to minimize the damage they do to you. You are unlikely to turn a glaring weakness into a strength, nor is it a good use of your limited time, energy, and willpower to try. You can, however, reduce such a liability substantially.
3. Recognize your remaining mild strengths and weaknesses for what they are and largely ignore them. The return on investment from trying to improve in these areas is almost non-existent. Your time is much better spent on steps 1 and 2.

Good Enough is Often Better

People whose goal is perfection in every decision are known as *maximizers*. Maximizers tend to be frustrated and unhappy because reality almost never meets their goals and expectations. They will spend a great deal of time on the decision-making process, and they will make some excellent decisions as a result. Unfortunately, they will never fully enjoy the fruits of their labors because their assessment is based on relative standards, not absolute ones. Their assessment is based relative to perfection, which is impossible to achieve.

Satisficers are the opposite of maximizers. They do not expect perfection from themselves, and they don't expect their decisions to be perfect. Satisficers set absolute standards, and when those standards have been met, they won't spend additional resources for incremental improvements. Satisficers are well aware of the point of diminishing returns; maximizers blow way past that point because they are obsessed with perfection.

Maximizers may make some better individual decisions than satisficers, but they also don't make some decisions that need to be made. They are preoccupied with making the best decision every time. Satisficers may give up a little on the quality of their decisions, but they more than make up for it in quantity. Satisficers will take care of all the business that needs to be taken care of and will still have a life.

Maximizers also suffer from an affliction that satisficers do not – buyer's remorse. Maximizers pay a price in mental anguish that satisficers rarely do. They also usually end up worse off financially than satisficers. Satisficers see the big picture and know when it's time to allocate resources to more productive endeavors. Maximizers are micro, not macro, and so they lose out on many opportunities because they can't see past their current obsession. Going back to the 80/20 rule, **satisficers are for more likely than maximizers to focus on the 20% of inputs that generates 80% of outcomes and ignore the rest.**

Success and failure have an emotional connection because two of our most powerful emotions are linked closely to them - success with happiness and failure with sadness. We naturally assume that when we are successful at something, happiness will immediately ensue. We also expect failure to bring sadness.

Because it is easier to generate negative emotions than positive ones and because we expect to feel sad when we fail, our expectations of sadness are almost always met. Ironically, one of the keys to success is to not let failure sadden you to the point of becoming discouraged. People like Thomas Edison failed far more often than they succeeded, yet ultimately such people are hailed as being extremely successful.

Success generating happiness is a much trickier proposition. People equate success with happiness, and they often use the terms synonymously. Achieving success can often prove disappointing, though. For example, a young woman may have a goal of reaching a certain management level at work. She may work long hours and make many sacrifices to climb the corporate ladder. Once the big promotion finally is received, she may experience more emptiness than elation. She may have the title, the salary, and the corner office. However, the rush of happiness she was expecting as part of the package isn't there because, contrary to popular expectations, happiness is not standard equipment on success. Also, because happiness did not come automatically, she can be left feeling not merely neutral but sad because her expectations were so unmet.

Success and failure are travelling companions. As you journey toward a goal, you will inevitably encounter both along the way. Harvard business professor Rosabeth Moss Kanter, who has studied many business organizations, observed: "Everything can look like failure in the middle." If you understand that failures along the way are an inevitable part of long-term success and if that recognition enables you to control the negative emotions that come along with those failures, you are much more likely to persevere to the point of eventual success.

When we begin a new challenge, we start out with many positive emotions - hope being perhaps the strongest of them all. Hope is an essential emotion in getting any project off the ground, but as Sir Francis Bacon observed, "Hope is a good breakfast, but it is a

6,000,000 MINUTES ON THE CLOCK

poor supper." Once the initial excitement at the beginning of the journey has waned and the long slog toward the finish line is all there is at the moment, we can become like kids in the back seat on a long drive - "Are we there yet? Are we there yet? Are we there yet?"

When a goal becomes closer to realization, our emotions improve, with confidence of success leading the way. There is a U-shape to the emotional pattern we encounter when we work toward a long-term goal - hope and anticipation at the beginning, confidence and pride toward the end, but a cornucopia of negative emotions in the middle, including but not limited to, anger, cynicism, depression, despair, impatience, stress, and uncertainty.

The onset of negative emotions is much less likely to slow us down, and they are also likely to be fewer and of lower intensity if we anticipate their arrival and prepare accordingly. Think about the pattern of going to college. At the beginning, you were full of hope and enthusiasm for this grand new experience you were about to have. Toward the end, you were focused on completing your degree with the pride and anticipation of becoming a college graduate. However, in between, there were three (or four or five) years of eight o'clock classes, boring lectures, ridiculously long term papers, and stressful weeks of final exams. For many college students, the hardest period begins around the second semester and lasts until the middle of junior year. In the second semester, there is not yet enough experience to have adjusted to the daily grind. By junior year, the student is both used to the daily grind and can see the light at the end of the tunnel. When students fail to complete their degree, that failure is not usually because of a lack of intelligence or even discipline, but rather an inability to handle the march through the valley of negative emotions.

What these students experience in that middle period is *growth*. The growth mindset is simply acknowledging that there will be failures, setbacks, bad feelings, and the rest. The growth is in the acceptance of all the negatives and then rising above them, even getting psyched up at the challenge of conquering the drudgery that comes with any job.

Knowing that we will face valleys along the way to our goals can actually make us optimistic. Knowing that failure is going to cross our path on the journey to success, we are more likely to seek it out and confront it, rather than fearing and avoiding it. It isn't the obstacle that we choose to face head-on that defeats us; it's the object that blindsides us because we refuse to acknowledge it.

The value of being an optimist has been articulated beautifully by Daniel Kahneman, the renowned psychologist and Nobel laureate:

"If you were allowed one wish for your child, seriously consider wishing him or her optimism. Optimists are normally cheerful and happy, and therefore popular; they are resilient in adapting to failures and hardships, their chances of clinical depression are reduced, their immune system is stronger, they take better care of their health, they feel healthier than others and are in fact likely to live longer. Optimistic individuals play a disproportionate role in shaping our lives. Their decisions make a difference; they are the inventors, the entrepreneurs, the political and military leaders - not average people."

6,000,000 MINUTES ON THE CLOCK

One of the keys to achieving anything worthwhile is persistence, and two of the benefits of an optimistic temperament are persistence in the face of obstacles and resilience in the face of setbacks. **If the first step in achieving a goal is the belief that you can and will achieve that goal, optimism is the first, most important tool to have in your kit.**

Optimism can be viewed as a cornucopia of positive emotions molded into a single personality. Those positive emotions and optimism have a convoluted cause and effect pattern. When you possess positive emotions like confidence, enthusiasm, and inner peace, it's easy to be an optimist. Going the other way, if you are a natural optimist, positive emotions like confidence, enthusiasm, and inner peace seem to pour forth like a natural spring. Whether you are a natural-born optimist or have made yourself into one, once you are one, the positive emotions seem almost self-generating.

Optimism can be taken to the extreme, though. Daniel Kahneman also points out that the blessings of optimism are offered only to individuals who are only mildly biased and who are able to accentuate the positive without losing track of reality. The overly optimistic person is likely to take excessive risks. How many fortunes have been lost because people refused to accurately assess or even acknowledge the downside potential of an investment? Every economic bubble that bursts is testament to the dangers over over-optimism. It is important to believe that you can handle a worst-case scenario, but in order for that belief to have value, you first have to be able to accurately gauge what the worst-case scenario actually is.

6,000,000 MINUTES ON THE CLOCK

WHAT ARE YOU THINKING?

In the 1984 movie *Moscow on the Hudson*, Robin Williams plays Vladimir Ivanov, a Soviet musician who defects to the U.S. The first third of the movie shows his life in Moscow – no freedom to choose where he will work or where he can go and waiting in long lines to get basic necessities like toilet paper.

When he goes to an American supermarket for the first time, Vladimir asks the manager where the "coffee line" is. He is informed there is no line, but that coffee is on aisle two. As he walks down the aisle, he recites the brand names he sees: *"Taster's Choice, decaffeinated, Maxwell House, El Pico, Chock Full o' Nuts, Espresso, Cappuccino, Café France, Sanka, Folgers, Café Caribe, coffee, coffee, coffee ,coffee, COFFEE!"*, at which point he passes out from hyperventilation.

The unbearability of no choice caused Vladimir to leave family, friends, and everything familiar for the chance to choose. His collapse in aisle two was a natural response when he became overloaded with choices (this was pre-Starbucks, too). In this situation, the effort required to make the right choice was totally out of whack with the potential benefits. Not to mention, Vladimir's choosing skills were underdeveloped.

Your life's work is a different story. The potential benefits make the effort of choosing wisely both necessary and worthwhile. Reading some books, taking some tests, and learning more about who you are and what you want is a small price to pay to discover a career direction that will provide more than a paycheck for the rest of your life.

6,000,000 MINUTES ON THE CLOCK

Risk and Reward

Change involves risk, which is why people have a reluctance to change, especially a change as important as their job. However, such risks are necessary because **risk and reward move in the same direction.** In order to earn a greater reward, you must be willing to assume greater risks. We understand this correlation when it comes to investing, but it also applies in other areas of life. Everyone who has ever been single understands that the reward of having a date on a Saturday night involves the risk of being rejected when you ask for a date.

Understanding your risk tolerance is essential in determining the rewards you will seek. **Your rewards are determined by your risk tolerance, not the other way around.** Commissioned sales people earn some of the highest incomes in any line of work. A lot of people would love to earn such an income. However, the risk of an income that can fluctuate wildly, in a job where a slump might cost you that job, is too much risk for most people to accept. That kind of pressure is one reason why such jobs have a high turnover rate.

There can be a huge difference between perceived risk and actual risk. We base decisions on our perceived risk. If we overestimate the risk, we are likely to freeze when we should act. If we underestimate the risk, we will act when we should freeze. Learning the facts about the risks we are taking narrows the gap between perceived and actual risk. We will still act based on perceived risk, but the closer our perception is to reality, the better our decisions will be.

People become more risk averse, perhaps too risk averse, when they are deciding among potential gains. The opposite is also true. When attempting to avoid a loss, we may be willing to accept too much risk to avoid the loss.

There is truth to the old saying that there is no one as free as someone with nothing left to lose. Let's say you've just lost your job; your home has been foreclosed on, and your spouse has left you. The risks involved in packing up your remaining possessions and heading off to another state or country, with no promises of anything, to start a new life and a new career in a new place seem small compared to the potential reward. On the other hand, if you still had your job, your house, and your spouse, making such a move with nothing solid at the other end would not likely happen. This form of loss is why, as people age and become established and successful, they tend to become more conservative. It's not political; it's psychological.

Psychological profiles, like those you get from the Myers-Briggs test, can be helpful in determining how much risk is within your comfort zone. While we can't change our essential personality, experience affects our perception of risk. Remember the first time you tried to dive off the diving board? You may have struggled for weeks to make that head-first plunge into the depths below. Once you succeeded, you asked yourself, "What was I so afraid of?" The best way to become less risk averse and a better judge of actual risk is to incrementally increase the risk you will take.

The Devil You Know

Despite our seemingly permanent contempt for politicians, incumbents are re-elected over 80% of the time. Our willingness to keep sending back the same people we vilify is an example of status quo bias. **When**

6,000,000 MINUTES ON THE CLOCK

there isn't a clearly superior alternative, we choose to stick to the status quo – the devil we know. Even when there is a better alternative out there, we often stick with the status quo because of the inconvenience of making the change and of that nagging uncertainty the change won't be for the better.

This status quo bias can lead us to not make job and career changes, even though we believe it would be better for us if we did. The idea of saying goodbye to co-workers, to familiar surroundings, to our daily routine is a lot to overcome. Who wants to go through the trouble of building all that up again when you have it here now?

Status quo bias can work the other way, though it occurs less frequently. Sometimes we develop a bias *against* the status quo. This bias tends to occur when we are bombarded with messages indicating our current situation isn't good enough. The goal is to stir discontent and to have us buy the product or service being offered. It takes a fairly high level of dissatisfaction for most people to dump the status quo. Those sales pitches are designed to ratchet up that level to the point of taking action.

At some point, you may have reached a tipping point with your job. At that point, you went from seeing the job in overall positive terms to seeing it in overall negative terms. The tipping point may have been reached as a result of a change in bosses, a change in job duties, or a change in physical environment. There may have also been a change in you. You outgrew the job. Your priorities changed as a result of a change outside of work (marriage, parenthood, etc.). Whatever the reasons, you are now focused on the CONS of your job instead of the PROS.

6,000,000 MINUTES ON THE CLOCK

"We're tunneling out after lunch – pass it on."

As you evaluate your current job situation, get out a sheet of paper and write PROS and CONS at the top of the page. Draw a line down the middle. Under the PROS column list everything positive about your job. List everything negative in the CONS column. Discuss your list with friends and family who can offer additional perspective (Bosses and gossipy co-workers should not be consulted.) This exercise will help you get the status quo into proper perspective.

(sample follows)

6,000,000 MINUTES ON THE CLOCK

Current job

PROS	CONS
short commute	bad neighborhood
good 401(k) plan	below-average salary
good health insurance	no life insurance
nice co-workers	obnoxious boss
no weekend work	some unpaid overtime
liberal sick leave	limited vacation time
low stress level	limited advancement
work is pleasant	work isn't stimulating

Trade-Ups and Trade-Offs

It's the Curse of the Desirable. It doesn't matter if you are desirable as a teammate, a lover, or an employee. If you are desirable, you have more choices available to you. Unfortunately, having more choices can actually make it harder to make the right choice.

If you are choosing between your current job and one other job, it's fairly easy to do a side-by-side comparison and determine which one is best for you. However, if you have your current job and three potential new jobs to choose from, the choices increase arithmetically, while the trade-offs increase geometrically.

These trade-offs are known as opportunity costs. Accepting one job costs you the opportunity to accept another job. The more choices you have, the higher the opportunity costs associated with that choice. When you go to Baskin-Robbins, you get 31 choices. That's good. You must reject 30 of them. That's bad.

The weight associated with rejecting alternatives tends to decrease our satisfaction with the choice we make. As we compare jobs, there's a tendency to start taking the best aspects from all these job opportunities and to create an ideal job out of them. This composite becomes the standard to which any choice we eventually make is compared. No real job can compare to that composite we make.

Once you've made your list of the PROS and CONS of your current job, prioritize each column. Prioritizing means listing in descending order what you like most and hate most about your job. The items at the top of the PROS list are items you definitely want to have at your new job. To lose those could make the new job worse by comparison, despite other improvements over the current situation.

The items at the top of your CONS list you don't want to take with you. However, some of those items may be part of almost any job (things like set hours or a dress code). It's important to discern the CONS items that are common to most any job and those that are unique to your current situation. The latter group you want to leave behind as much as possible.

If you think you will find a job with all the PROS of your current job (plus a few more) and none of the CONS, wake up. Unless you stumble across a job that constantly feeds your ego and wallet, while allowing you to avoid any contact with humans displaying negative traits, you are going to have trade-offs.

When evaluating PROS and CONS, think of them as chess pieces. The PROS are your team; the CONS are the opponent. When you prioritize the list, you assign a rank to each item. Some are queens; some are knights, and some are pawns. The items at the bottom of the list are pawns. In chess, you readily exchange one of your pawns for one of your opponent's pawns; so it should be with the low items on the list. Getting rid of a minor CON is consolation for getting rid of a minor PRO.

6,000,000 MINUTES ON THE CLOCK

The bigger pieces require more consideration. Are you willing to trade off your top PRO to get rid of your top CON (an exchange of queens)? The top items on your list may also have greater ramifications for others. For example, the top PRO may be a large salary, but the top CON may be constant travel. Someone with small children at home would have to weigh the impact of such trade-offs on family as well.

When we are evaluating a new job versus our current one, there is a tendency to underestimate the CONS of the new job. This underestimation occurs in part because we never know all the CONS of a job until we spend some time on that job. Also, when we are anxious to make a job change, there is a natural tendency to play up the PROS and play down the CONS to justify the decision to make the job change. It's important to be aware of this tendency for two reasons – first, you don't want to make a job change based on an erroneous evaluation. Second, awareness of this tendency can reduce your chances of "buyer's remorse", after you settle into your new job and realize it isn't a paid Utopia.

Going Solo

You're suffocating. There are the endless, useless meetings, the moronic co-workers, the bi-polar boss, the time-sapping emails, the lack of direction, the lack of progress, and the lack of purpose. Sometimes you feel you just can't take another day of it. You want to spread your wings and fly like an eagle and not waste another day with these turkeys.

Don't start flapping your wings yet. Before you take the tremendously huge step of venturing out on your own, there are a lot of questions to answer and a lot of work to be done.

The first thing you will need to do is determine your motives for wanting to go on your own. If the main motivation is to get away from something – if you feel pushed in that direction, Stop! That push may be sufficient motivation to give two weeks' notice, but it will not be sufficient motivation to succeed in an environment where the failure rate hovers around 75% in the first year.

Negative emotions are a drain of energy, not a source of energy. It is negative emotions that push you away from your current situation. To succeed in starting a business from scratch, you need positive emotions, which are a source of energy. You get that energy when you feel pulled toward something; when it feels like a calling, your destiny.

If you are going to fly solo, you need to be pulled, not pushed to do it. You have to *need* to do it, not merely *want* to do it.

Low, Medium, or High Risk?

There are different methods to being on your own, with different risks and benefits. One of the first things to determine is which method is appropriate for you and your circumstances.

At the low end of the risk scale is the ***independent contractor***, someone found commonly in technical fields. They are often sub-contracted by an agency and will work for a single company until a project is completed or until the funding dries up.

An independent contractor often has the worst of both worlds. They have to look and act like employees of the hiring party, as many outside of the company don't know they aren't employees. While they may have slightly more flexibility than an employee in the method of completing a task, they are still under the control of the hiring party. Their duration of contract is at the discretion of the hiring party, and there is no safety net when they find themselves suddenly without work. There are also none of the employee benefits like health insurance, 401(k) plans, paid vacation, etc. Lack of benefits is why an independent contractor is often paid more on an hourly basis than an employee counterpart.

An independent contractor arrangement can work well for someone who wants a more flexible work arrangement, or for someone who is already retired, or for someone who has a working spouse, where in such cases necessities like health insurance are already provided.

Next up on the risk-reward scale is the *small business owner*, which is a more complex structure than an independent contractor.

When you start a small business, you first need a business plan. That plan will include a market analysis of potential customers and competition, marketing and sales plans, expense and income projections, pro forma financial statements, and physical housing for the business.

You will need all this information in order to get financing to help get your business off the ground. Conventional outside financing will require this data and more, and they will charge an interest rate commensurate with the risk, which they consider to be high. If financing is coming from private sources (like family), you still need to have a solid business plan, since they also need to have their interests protected. You don't want to lose your family, as well as your business, through a faulty plan. Even if all the money to start a business is coming out of your own pocket, you owe yourself the same due diligence you would owe to a third-party lender.

The business owner, unlike the independent contractor, has the opportunity to build something of market value, something with the ability to someday generate income without the direct labor of the owner. That growth generally takes many years and a lot of dealings with customers, employees, and creditors in the interim. There is more long-term potential for wealth than being an independent contractor, but there is a longer gestation period.

At the top of the risk-reward continuum is the *entrepreneur*. While many, if not most, people who are out on their own consider themselves to be entrepreneurs, few actually meet the true definition.

It's Not What They Do; It's Who They Are

Every entrepreneur I've ever met, regardless of their enterprise, takes a cue from the commander of another Enterprise, Captain Kirk. The entrepreneur longs to "boldly go where no man has gone before."

The entrepreneur, more than anyone else, is a person with *vision.* Our history is replete with them – Benjamin Franklin, Thomas Edison, Henry Ford, and Steve Jobs, to name a few. They each had ideas for a future no one could even imagine. After their genius and determination made their vision reality, we all wondered how the rest of us could have missed something so obvious. The entrepreneur has a right brain that puts the rest of us to shame.

6,000,000 MINUTES ON THE CLOCK

What makes a great entrepreneur? According to Silicon Valley venture capitalist John Doerr, the best ones are "missionaries, not mercenaries."

"Mercenaries have a lot of drive, they're opportunistic and always pitching their latest deal, whereas missionaries are more passionate and strategic. Mercenaries are sprinting and often have in their organizations an aristocracy of founders, whereas the missionaries are in it for the long run, obsessing on customers, not competition. They try to build a meritocracy—a loud, noisy place where the best ideas can get on the table."

Most entrepreneurs demonstrated their tendencies at an early age. They would often start a business like mowing lawns, baby-sitting, or delivering newspapers. These early enterprises are also where most of them learned about money and its importance in making and sustaining a successful business.

Entrepreneurs are competitive by nature, but their competition is most often themselves. They are less interested in how they are doing compared to others than how they are doing compared to the standards they have set for themselves.

Entrepreneurs don't worry much about what others think. They recognize that most people don't possess their sense of vision, so those opinions aren't of much value. Entrepreneurs value integrity; they will do business on a handshake, and they feel strong associations with people who share their work ethic. Henry Ford and Thomas Edison were close friends because they were so similar.

Entrepreneurs don't retire. **You retire from what you do, not from who you are.** When one venture has reached the desired level of success, they start looking for the next challenge. Often, they have different projects going on simultaneously.

Entrepreneurs work hard; they give their all to their endeavors, but they are actually better than most when it comes to maintaining balance in their lives. They value time with family, and they can usually afford leisure activities that are out of reach for most people.

Entrepreneurs are satisficers, not maximizers, which means they recognize when effort has reached the point of diminishing returns, and they move on. They know instinctively when it's "good enough" and are satisfied. A maximizer will obsess about something until it's perfect. The entrepreneur recognizes that perfection is not the goal; the goal is maximum productivity.

Entrepreneurs are, above all, agents of change.

6,000,000 MINUTES ON THE CLOCK

A Calculated Leap of Faith

Unfortunately, there is no standardized test you can take to determine if you are an entrepreneur, or even if you should go into business for yourself. That's a call you have to make after some serious introspection. Many people take such a leap and fail, not because they had a bad idea, but because they didn't make sure there were the tools in place to enable them to succeed. It's sad to see someone fail when they take a leap they shouldn't have taken. It's sadder still to see someone who should have taken that leap, but couldn't bring themselves to do it. They and the world are worse off for that great idea that never got its chance.

It starts with an idea. The idea must be something that is unique and/or better than what is currently out there. Sometimes the idea is amazing in its simplicity. Ray Kroc's idea was that, for the low-priced dining out experience, consistency is more important to the consumer than getting the best meal. The product he created was McDonald's.

The product of your idea must be able to be described in terms of benefits to the consumer. The tendency of the producer is to focus on the features of a product. However, you should **begin with intended benefits to the customer and let the features evolve to meet those benefits.** The customer seeks benefits, not features, so focus your product's promotion on benefits.

Know your target market, not just demographically, but psychologically. You certainly need to know the hard numbers of your market – age, income, location, etc. That information tells you the *breadth* of your market. You also need to know the emotional reasons they want your product. That information tells you the *depth* of your market, which is important to be able to assess consumer loyalty. If there is no emotional attachment to your product or service over another's, you will lose to the lower price or new features of a competitor.

Other than coming up with a killer idea, the single biggest obstacle to launching a successful enterprise is cash flow. A great idea may generate investors, but for every budding entrepreneur with too much investment capital, there are a thousand with too little.

A well-thought out business plan can give you an idea of the business' cash flow needs, and that business plan is essential to lure bona fide investors. However, a business plan is an estimate at best. There is a tendency to underestimate expenses and start-up delays and to overestimate the speed and volume of income. A good business plan should be able to stand up to the scrutiny of someone less optimistic (more realistic?) than you.

It isn't just the cash flow of the business; the cash flow of your household needs serious planning. At the very least, you are likely to be giving up a part of the household income to make this leap. That loss will require a downward adjustment in household expenses to keep the household financially solvent. If you are stopping a paycheck that was providing 50% of your household income and if your expenses were already at 90% of your household income, where will you make the necessary cuts to balance the budget? Too often, people cover this shortfall with an increase in personal debt. When the income from the business doesn't materialize quickly or sufficiently enough, the debt load can send the budding entrepreneur into personal bankruptcy.

There is an old saying - Overnight success takes

about fifteen years. Experience proves that time frame is about right. Sure, the Google Guys became billionaires in less than half that time, but let's stick to reality here.

There are going to be trade-offs getting your idea off the ground. You will have to make allocation decisions about time, money, energy, production, marketing, research, and other things you can't yet imagine. This volume of decision making means one of your most important skills is the ability to make a decision and then let it run.

There is a decision hierarchy, and at the top of that hierarchy are decisions affecting your life, as well as the lives of your family. If you have a family and if they are not willing to make the sacrifices necessary to make your venture succeed, you are at a fatal disadvantage. It's hard enough making this transition, even with the full support of those closest to you. If you can't convince them that this venture is worth the sacrifice, how will you convince others?

So, before you put together a business plan, you need to put together a ***life plan***. Start with the kind of life that makes you feel happy and fulfilled. Yes, those are fuzzy terms, but you know what makes you feel that way. The desire for happiness and fulfillment is also the best motivator one could have.

As you put together your life plan, here are some questions you should ask yourself (and ask yourself any other questions you feel are relevant):
- What kinds of activities give me the greatest sense of satisfaction?
- What do I have to offer that other people want and need?
- With what kind of people do I enjoy spending time?
- How much money do I need (not how much money do

6,000,000 MINUTES ON THE CLOCK

I want)?
- Where would I choose to live?
- What are my obligations to others?
- How can I meet those obligations and still fulfill my dreams?
- If I found out I had one week to live, what would I most regret that I didn't do.
- If I found out I had six months to live, what would I make sure I did in that remaining time?

Any business venture you put together should have as its primary goal the ability to help you achieve your life goals. Simply stated, **your work supports your life, not the other way around.** When we get swamped by the details and demands of our work, we can easily forget the proper order of things.

Whatever business you create, make sure it is one that reflects you and your values. Your business should appear as an extension of you, which will make it easier for you to run the business, rather than having the business run you.

Burning Bridges

The more non-reversible a decision seems, the more difficult it becomes to make, which is one reason why making a major new commitment, like marriage or a new job, is so hard.

There can be a great temptation when you leave a job to take a few parting shots at annoying co-workers, and especially at your soon-to-be-ex-boss. Don't do it! First, it serves no purpose other than juvenile ego gratification. Second, you may need some of these people in the future – as references, as contacts, maybe even as customers.

Third, knowing you didn't burn the bridge back to your old job can make the decision to take a new job a little easier to make. The bridge back makes it possible for you to move forward with less fear.

At this point, a disclaimer is needed. While keeping bridges intact can enable you to make a needed change, there is a psychological toll. (In the journey of life, all bridges are toll bridges.) Having options, especially the option of returning to the status quo, can keep us from making the psychological commitment to succeed at our new job.

Consider the phrase "til death do us part." The weight of a commitment like that should make one cautious in saying "I do." Those who take it seriously are more likely to do what it takes to make the marriage succeed than those who view divorce as an easy option if things don't work out according to plan. **The downside to options is that we are less likely to commit the necessary effort to succeed at the option we've chosen.** When his junior officers doubted they could press on in the Battle of the Bulge, General Patton sternly admonished them saying, "If we are not victorious, let no one come back alive!" That's commitment!

In the short term, we tend to regret the things we did that didn't turn out well more than we regret the things we didn't do that might have turned out well. Yet, over time, we regret more the things we *didn't* do more than the things we did. We chastise ourselves over our sins of omission more than over our sins of commission. When we don't take advantage of the opportunity of a lifetime, even though that opportunity involves risks, we often spend the better part of a lifetime regretting our lack of faith and courage.

6,000,000 MINUTES ON THE CLOCK

If you ask old people about their biggest regrets, they'll tell you of the trips they didn't take, the time they didn't spend with their kids, the "I Love You" they didn't say when they had the chance. When you are contemplating a major life change like a new career, it can be very useful to ask the advice of someone much older and wiser than you. If there are such people in your life who do not have a personal stake in your contemplated change, see what they think about your plans.

Finally, don't think you will kick yourself for the rest of your life if you attempt to make a better life for yourself, and it just doesn't quite work out as planned. In such a case, you may have some regrets in the short term, but over time, you will be glad you took the risk. Failure in a noble cause is still noble.

6,000,000 MINUTES ON THE CLOCK

6,000,000 MINUTES ON THE CLOCK

WHERE DO YOU THINK YOU'RE GOING?

The best-selling book *Good to Great* chronicles what companies do to go from being merely good to being great. The first thing great companies do is to get the right people on the bus and the wrong people off the bus. Then those people decide where to take the bus. The point in *Good to Great* is that the selection of the right employees to ride the "bus" is the biggest factor in an organization's success.

Also, average companies give employees something to work on. Great companies give employees something to work toward. Great companies offer a place to go, not just a plan to follow.

Catch the Right Bus

You're being invited onto the bus. Hopefully, you are being invited onto more than one bus. How do you know if the drivers are competent, if the other passengers are easy to get along with, if the bus is well-maintained, and if the bus is going where you want to go, and if it is even seeking your input as to its destination?

Too often, in the excitement of receiving a job offer, we don't ask these and similar questions about our new situation. We assume everything is fine because we so badly want it to be.

You need to evaluate a new employer even more than they need to evaluate you, and here's why. You will be one of dozens, hundreds, maybe thousands of employees at your new job. Your individual impact, especially in the early years there, will not be earth-shaking. On the other hand, you are about to decide on the one job you will have for the foreseeable future. The job will provide you not only with an income, but also with future opportunities for growth and a sizeable part of your personal identity. You've got more on the line in this merger than they do. You owe it to yourself to evaluate them at least as hard as they evaluate you.

Before you can say yes to a job offer, you should be able to answer these questions about the job and the employer:
- Why am I here?
- Why should I go with you instead of your competitor?
- What can I do for you?
- What problems of yours can I help solve?
- What kind of organization are you?
- Do you have the corporate personality and values that fit with mine?
- Can you afford me? In other words, can you pay me enough to beat the competition, but still have it be less money than my new boss makes?
- What does this job involve?
- What are the skills a top employee in this job would have to have?
- Do I want to work with these people?
- Is the product or service your company produces something that can make me proud?
- Are you a leader in your field, or at least aspire to be?

Revolving Doors

As you decide if a company is one you want to join, one of the best tools to use is the company's retention ratio or turnover ratio. These are simply opposite ratios of each other – retention ratio states the percentage of employees who stayed over the last year; turnover ratio states the percentage who left. From here on we'll refer to turnover ratio only. A company's Human Resources department should be able to provide you with data on turnover ratios for the industry and your particular job and how they compare to that average.

An employer's turnover ratio may tell you more than any other statistic about the work environment there. When a company is trying to get you onboard, they will tell you all the good things about the company – salary, benefits, opportunity, pleasant work environment, etc. The turnover ratio tells you with total objectivity whether the people in charge know what they're doing. People leave bosses more than they leave companies or jobs. When the bosses don't know what they're doing, the employees are keenly aware of it, and they don't stick around.

Turnover ratios vary widely by industry, so it's important to know the turnover ratio for the industry you are entering. The average employee turnover rate nationally is about 15%, which means 15% of positions have to be filled every year. That rate also means the average employee changes jobs every 7 years. As a rule, the higher the level of training and education required for a position, the lower the turnover ratio tends to be. When you invest a lot of years to reach a position, you don't walk away on a whim.

A low turnover ratio will imply the following about a company (A high ratio will imply just the opposite.):
- Management is competent and communicates clear expectations to the employees.
- Management provides feedback to employees and makes them feel valued.
- Employees feel free to speak their mind and criticize

within the goal of making improvements in the company, product, or service.
- Employees are encouraged to demonstrate skills and talents, even if they are outside their normal duties.
- Raises and promotions are merit-based with criteria for them clearly stated.
- If an employee's behavior or performance becomes unacceptable, they are terminated quickly, to protect the morale of the other employees.

While some turnover is desirable because it brings new people and ideas into the organization and keeps everyone from ending up at the top of the pay scale, organizations want to have a low turnover ratio. Replacing an employee costs a company, on average, three months' salary of the replacement. For top executive positions, it can cost a year's salary or more. The only reason a company would want to have a high turnover ratio is to keep salaries as low as possible by having many employees at the bottom of the pay scale. Productivity and morale would both be poor at such a place. Avoid such organizations altogether.

Are You Worth It?

The amount that you can be paid for your work is directly affected by the price that can be obtained for the product or service you produce. That price falls within a range. The producer's cost creates the floor of price. Any business that charges a price that is less than its cost of production won't be in business for long. Labor costs are typically the highest single business expense. For most businesses, they comprise at least half of total expenses, and can be as high as ninety percent in service industries.

6,000,000 MINUTES ON THE CLOCK

For that reason, changes in employee compensation have a major impact on pricing. The higher the compensation structure, the higher the price floor must be to be a profitable venture.

The value of the product or service to the consumer creates the ceiling of price. Sometimes that value can be objectively measured. If a service you provide saves a customer $1,000, paying only $500 for that service is an obvious, objective gain for the customer. Sometimes the value is more subjective. A Starbucks coffee is considerably more expensive than a Waffle House coffee. Those who value only the coffee aren't likely to pay the higher Starbucks price. However, there's a subjective value to the Starbucks experience, at least for many people. That experience creates value for those Starbucks customers; at least enough value to justify the price premium of Starbucks over its competitors.

When a new product or service is created, the perceived value is likely to be high. Pricing at this stage is governed by the ceiling more than the floor. Businesses frequently lose money in the early stages of a product/service life cycle because they are recouping development costs and sales volume is starting at zero. There is also little or no competition at this stage, so prices can be raised until there is measurable sales resistance.

Any highly profitable business enterprise will draw competitors like bees to flowers. New competitors will typically compete on price, driving down prices and profitability. As downward pressure on prices continues, profit margins get squeezed. Since raising prices under these conditions will decimate sales, profitability is increased by reducing costs – lowering the floor. Since labor costs are typically the biggest cost, employee compensation is affected, by wage and hiring freezes, or by layoffs and wage reductions under severe conditions.

Competition, and barriers to entry by competition, are key factors in determining profitability, and hence the wage structure. Brain surgeons make more than janitors for two main reasons. First, the value of having a brain tumor removed is greater than the value of having your office cubicle cleaned. Second, the arduous path to become a brain surgeon means there are few qualified to do it. In other words, brain surgeons don't have cut-throat competition for business. The path to becoming a janitor is far less arduous. There are so many potential janitors out there that wages will never be any higher than is necessary to attract enough janitors to meet the demand for them.

The professions that offer the best chances for higher incomes and relative job security are those that offer real value to the customer (objectively and subjectively measured) and that can't easily attract competitors and imitators. By the way, competition comes in many forms, from people in another country to software that hasn't been invented yet. If it can be done cheaper, eventually it will be.

Money and More

If you are reading this book with the purpose of learning how to get paid more, this is the section of interest to you. But remember, **more money will not make you love a job, any more than it would make you love a person.** Money is one way your employer demonstrates their appreciation of your contributions. Money can enable you to buy more stuff, but money has very little connection to job satisfaction. If you think you will love a job you hate if you are just paid more, you're fooling yourself. The rush of a raise will soon fade. You will spend up to your new income level and then feel even more trapped in a job you now hate even more. You will realize you sold out instead of doing something you love.

The purpose of a company's compensation system is, or should be, to get and keep the best people. It should not attempt to get right behavior from the wrong people.

For the average employee, benefit costs as a percentage of total compensation run around 30%. That figure means that if a company is paying an employee $35,000 a year, they are also paying another $15,000 for the benefits that employee receives.

There are legally mandated insurance and benefits a company must provide and pay for in whole or part. These mandates include social security, workers' compensation, and unemployment insurance.

The most common employee benefits offered by small businesses are:
- Paid Vacations; offered by 75% of small businesses.*
- Employee Health Insurance Plan; 61%
- Paid Sick Leave; 59%
- Disability Insurance; 41%
- Education Reimbursement for Job; 39%
- Pension Plan; 30%
- Life Insurance; 29%
- Dental Insurance; 24% *

*provided to full-time staff with at least 1 year's service.

Benefits can be broken down into two broad categories: nice-to-have and need-to-have. Need-to-have benefits include any insurance coverage and retirement plans. Retirement plans are so important and complex they are covered in a later chapter.

Health insurance is probably the single most important benefit to the majority of U.S. workers. No one, regardless of age or health, can afford to be without it. Health insurance is often the main reason employees don't leave a company. They may have a medical condition that would preclude them from coverage at a new job or out on their own.

The complexities of different types of coverage are beyond our scope here. Here is what you need to know – any company worth working for should make group health insurance available for employees and have it available for a reasonable premium. **You must have this coverage.** To go without health insurance when it's available, to put that kind of financial risk on yourself and your family, with the only benefit being the saving of the insurance premium, demonstrates a level of irresponsibility that should make you unacceptable to any decent employer.

Disability insurance pays you in the event you are unable to perform your job due to injury or illness. It is one of those benefits that younger people don't give much thought. However, if you become disabled and can't work, your income goes away, but your expenses don't go away. In many cases, expenses increase significantly with a disability. At least if you die, your expenses die with you. The loss of income without the loss of expenses is why disability insurance is even more necessary than life insurance. There's another reason, too. If you are under forty, you are twenty times more likely to be disabled before reaching retirement age than you are to die.

Long-term disability insurance (which usually begins

six months after being disabled and can cover from three years up to age sixty-five) is relatively inexpensive. It typically pays about two-thirds of what your salary was at the time of the disability. (If they paid more than two-thirds, you'd be less motivated to get well and return to work.) Because of the risk of becoming disabled and the cost if you do, you should enroll in this coverage if your employer makes it available. Generally, all but the smallest organizations offer this coverage as part of their benefits package.

Life insurance is necessary if there are others who depend on your income. Dependent children and non-working spouses certainly fit that description. The death benefit from life insurance would be used by your survivors to replace the income lost by your untimely demise.

Employers, through an insurer, often offer life insurance at a lower price, known as group rates. There may be a requirement by the insurer that a minimum percentage of employees sign up to have the coverage available. The insurer doesn't want only higher-risk employees getting the coverage and messing up all their risk calculations.

There is usually a small amount of coverage (perhaps one year's salary) that you can get without any medical exam. Higher amounts of coverage may require you to qualify medically. Each company and each insurer will vary on what they offer and how they offer it.

The advantages of group life insurance through an employer are lower premiums compared to getting the coverage on your own and no qualifying medical exam for at least some of the offered coverage. The disadvantage is that you typically can't take the coverage with you when you leave. The insurer may offer you coverage on an individual policy, but that's not usually any different than what you could get on the open market.

Dental coverage is excluded from most health insurance policies, which is why you see it offered separately. For all the reasons you need health insurance, you need dental insurance, too.

For both dental and health insurance, policies that pay for preventive care, such as regular dental cleanings and exams, are better. An employer who encourages employees to take care of themselves demonstrates concern for the employees' well-being. They are also protecting their investment, as healthy employees are more productive employees.

Paid vacation and sick leave policies don't vary as widely from company to company as other benefits, in part because everyone seems to check those out first. In asking about benefits, you should ask about vacation and sick days last. Otherwise, it may look like you want to get away from the job before you even have it.

Before you get excited at the prospect of extra vacation time, check to see how many hours a week you'll be expected to put in at your new job. When you're paid a salary, as opposed to an hourly wage, it's much easier for your boss to squeeze you for more hours. If you're working fifty hours a week, you would need an extra ten weeks of vacation to be even with someone working forty hours a week. Giving you an extra week of vacation to squeeze ten more weeks of work out of you is a good deal for your employer, but not for you.

Any company that encourages continuing education by paying for it gets a gold star. Good employers recognize that offering tuition reimbursement and the like is not an expense, it's an investment.

Because of the pace of change now, it is essential that all employees at all levels continuously expand their base of knowledge. The employees who take advantage of such benefits not only keep up to date and are more secure in their current jobs, they can also accumulate credentials necessary for the next job up the ladder.

Many companies provide reimbursement for education expenses after you satisfactorily complete a class or a program. That's perfectly acceptable and to be expected. In business you pay for results, not for mere effort.

Profit-sharing and ESOP's (employee stock ownership plans) are nice to have, but don't put too much weight on them. Profit as defined for profit-sharing plans can be rather fuzzy, and management often has a lot of discretion in deciding if there will be profit-sharing each year.

Look to see if there is a solid history of corporate profitability and if the company has shared that with employees as agreed. Whatever you do, don't base any decisions, whether to accept a job or even making up a budget, on the assumption that profit sharing will materialize. If it comes, let it be a pleasant surprise.

ESOP's give you the chance to buy stock in your employer company, usually at a discount of 10-15%. There is often a requirement that you hold the stock for a minimum period; you can't buy, sell immediately and reap a quick profit. It's important to remember that you already have a lot invested with your employer. It's wise not to put too many eggs in one basket. It's much more important that you fully fund your retirement program (need-to-have) than participate in an ESOP (nice-to-have).

6,000,000 MINUTES ON THE CLOCK

How They Rank & How They Rank 'Em

U.S. News & World Report - January, 2015

Choosing an occupation is personal, and of course, there is no ideal way to determine the best job overall. Still, U.S. News' Best Jobs rankings offer job seekers an intuitive method to compare professions based on components that matter most: salary, the number of expected openings, advancement opportunities and career fulfillment. The result of our efforts is a list of jobs ranked according to their ability to meet those employment concerns.

The Best Jobs methodology is divided into two components: how U.S. News selects jobs to profile, and how those jobs are ranked against each other.

Selecting the Jobs

To identify professions that should be included in the 2015 rankings, we started with data on jobs with the greatest hiring demand, or in other words, the highest projected number of openings from 2012 to 2022, as categorized by the U.S. Bureau of Labor Statistics. The jobs at the top of the list were then selected for the 2015 Best Jobs analysis and rankings.

Ranking the Jobs

U.S. News ranks jobs in an overall list and in six mutually exclusive, occupational industry lists: Best Business Jobs, Best Creative Jobs, Best Construction Jobs, Best Health Care Jobs, Best Social Services Jobs and Best Technology Jobs. Professions are ranked based on our calculated overall score, which combines several components into a single weighted average score between 0 and 5.

The overall score is calculated from seven component measures, and for each measure, jobs receive a score between 0 and 10. Here are the component measures and their weights in computing the overall score:
-10-Year Growth Volume (10 percent)
-10-Year Growth Percentage (10 percent)
-Median Salary (30 percent)
-Job Prospects (20 percent)
-Employment Rate (20 percent)
-Stress Level (5 percent)
-Work-Life Balance (5 percent)

About the Component Measures

1. 10-year growth volume. Growth volume, according to the BLS, is the total number of new jobs that should be created for an occupation in a 10-year timespan. For example, the BLS projects the United States will add 23,300 new dentist jobs between 2012 and 2022.

Why is it important?
An occupation with significant job growth is likely to have many new job opportunities in the future. This is also a crucial factor, because we use the BLS' projected growth volume to select the jobs we'll rank each year.

How is this score calculated?
We translate job growth volumes from a number to a score of up to 10 points. Those occupations expected to grow by 500,000 openings or more received the highest score: 10. Occupations with job growth numbers

6,000,000 MINUTES ON THE CLOCK

between 200,000 and 499,999 earned 8 points; between 100,000 and 199,999 earned 6 points; less than 100,000 openings earned 4 points; and any occupations for which numbers were expected to decrease received 2 points.

2. 10-year growth percentage. This is an occupation's employment percentage growth over the course of 10 years. For example, the BLS estimate of 23,300 new dentist jobs between 2012 and 2022 equates to 15.9 percent.

Why is it important?
The 10-year growth percentage measures how rapidly an occupation is expanding. A high growth rate indicates strengthening demand for this type of worker. The BLS predicts that total employment is projected to increase 10.8 percent between 2012 and 2022. Those jobs with higher percentages are growing faster than average. Growth percentage is also important to our methodology, because the growth rate is used to select the jobs we'll rank each year.

How is this score calculated?
We translate job growth percentages from a number to a score of up to 10 points. Occupations for which the projected growth rate increased by 30 percent or more earned the total possible 10 points; those for which growth increased between 20 and 29 percent earned 8 points; where growth increased between 10 and 19 percent, the job earned 6 points; and where growth increased by 9 percent or less, the job earned 4 points. Any occupations that saw growth decrease received 2 points.

6,000,000 MINUTES ON THE CLOCK

3. Median salary. This is the median salary earned by someone employed in a given occupation, according to BLS.

Why is it important?
Most people prefer higher salaries.

How is this score calculated?
We translate median salary from a dollar amount to a numerical score using the following formula: salary score = the square root of the median salary divided by 40. We set a maximum salary score of 10 points.

4. Employment rate. The percentage of people in an occupation who are currently employed.

Why is it important?
It's more challenging to get a job in an occupation with high unemployment.

How is this score calculated?
We translate unemployment rates, recorded for each profession, to a 10-point scale. For example, if a job's unemployment rate is 4 percent or less, it earned the full possible 10 points; a job with unemployment between 4.1 percent and 6 percent earned 8 points; between 6.1 and 8 percent earned 6 points; between 8.1 and 10 percent earned 4 points; and those jobs with unemployment higher than 10 percent earned 2 points.

5. Future job prospects. This rating indicates the ease of landing a job in the future, based on the number of openings versus the number of job seekers. For example, the BLS predicts nurse practitioners will be in high demand, particularly in underserved inner cities and rural areas, so this job has an excellent job prospect rating. By contrast, the BLS projects there will be more students graduating from law school each year than there are jobs available. Competition for open positions for **lawyers** will be competitive, so this occupation received a lower job prospect rating.

Why is it important?
If you want to pursue a career in which the BLS projects it will be easier to find employment over the next 10 years, aim for one with a higher job prospect rating.

How is this score calculated?
We translate the BLS "descriptive rating" to a score of up to 10 points. A job that received an "excellent" prospect rating earned 10 points; a job that has a "good" rating earned 8 points; a job with a "favorable" rating earned 6 points; and an occupation with a "keen competition" rating earned a score of 4. Jobs for which prospects weren't identified or for which prospects varied were considered not applicable for a prospect score by U.S. News.

6. Stress level. This rating indicates the amount of day-to-day stress someone might experience while working in an occupation.

Why is it important?
The level of stress an individual feels in his or her job can lower quality of life, negatively affect health and alter someone's opinion of the work he or she does.

How is this score calculated?

6,000,000 MINUTES ON THE CLOCK

Based on interviews and extensive research, our editors assign qualitative stress-level ratings to each occupation. These ratings are intended to represent the average stress level for the occupation, and it's important to note that stress varies significantly among individuals and their specific job circumstances.

These qualitative stress-level ratings are translated on a 10-point scale. A stress level rating of "High" translates to 2 points (the lowest score); a rating of "Above Average" translates to 4 points; a rating of "Average" translates to 6 points; "Below Average" to 8 points; and "Low" translates to 10 points (the highest score).

7. Work-life balance. This rating captures how much any profession will affect lifestyle.

Why is it important?
Finding the appropriate balance between career, ambition, health, family and leisure activities can improve job performance.

How is this score calculated?
Based on interviews and an assessment of literature, U.S. News editors assign qualitative work-life balance ratings for each occupation. Similar to stress level, it's important to note that work-life balance may vary significantly among individuals and with specific job circumstances.

Our qualitative work-life balance ratings are translated to scores on a 10-point scale. A rating of "High" translates to 10 points (the highest score); a rating of "Above Average" translates to 8 points; a rating of "Average" translates to 6 points; a rating of "Below Average" translates to 4 points; and a rating of "Low" translates to 2 points (the lowest score).

6,000,000 MINUTES ON THE CLOCK

U.S. News & World Report 100 Best Jobs 2015

1. Dentist
2. Nurse Practitioner
3. Software Developer
4. Physician
5. Dental Hygienist
6. Physical Therapist
7. Computer Systems Analyst
8. Information Security Analyst
9. Registered Nurse
10. Physician Assistant
11. Web Developer
12. Diagnostic Medical Sonographer
13. Occupational Therapist
14. Market Research Analyst
15. Marketing Manager
16. Accountant
17. School Psychologist
18. Mechanical Engineer
19. Occupational Therapy Assistant
20. Operations research Analyst
21. IT Manager
22. Civil Engineer
23. Cost Estimator
24. Esthetician
25. Financial Adviser
26. Logistician
27. Pharmacist
28. Medical Equipment Repairer
29. Dietitian and Nutritionist
30. Speech-Language Pathologist
31. Computer Systems Administrator
32. Radiologic Technologist

6,000,000 MINUTES ON THE CLOCK

33. Insurance Agent
34. Database Administrator
35. Marriage and Family Therapist
36. Epidemiologist
37. Construction Manager
38. Substance Abuse Counselor
39. Elementary School Teacher
40. Bookkeeping, Accounting and Auditing Clerk
41. Licensed Practical/Vocational Nurse
42. Optician
43. High School Teacher
44. Loan Officer
45. Middle School Teacher
46. Physical Therapist Assistant
47. Business Operations Manager
48. Pharmacy Technician
49. Home Health Aide
50. HR Specialist
51. Respiratory Therapist
52. Nail Technician
53. Lawyer
54. Medical Secretary
55. Maintenance and Repair Worker
56. Veterinarian
57. Meeting, Convention and Event Planner
58. Sales Manager
59. Personal Care Aide
60. Administrative Assistant
61. Sales Representative
62. Massage Therapist
63. Computer Programmer
64. Veterinary Technologist and Technician
65. Financial Analyst
66. Hairdresser

6,000,000 MINUTES ON THE CLOCK

67. Dental Assistant
68. Management Analyst
69. Financial Manager
70. Clinical Social Worker
71. Medical Assistant
72. Medical Health Counselor
73. Police Officer
74. Recreation and Fitness Worker
75. Public Relations Specialist
76. School Counselor
77. Computer Support Specialist
78. Real Estate Agent
79. Plumber
80. Clinical Laboratory Technician
81. Architect
82. Surgical Technologist
83. Auto Mechanic
84. Compliance Officer
85. Exterminator
86. Child and Family Social Worker
87. Art Director
88. Preschool Teacher
89. Interpreter and Translator
90. Security Guard
91. Paralegal
92. Executive Assistant
93. Taxi Driver and Chauffeur
94. Paramedic
95. Customer Service Representative
96. Sheet Metal Worker
97. Bill Collector
98. Office Clerk
99. Teacher Assistant
100. Receptionist

6,000,000 MINUTES ON THE CLOCK

CNN/Money 100 Best Jobs 2015

	JOB TITLE	MEDIAN PAY	10-YR. JOB GROWTH
1.	Software Architect	$124,000	23%
2.	Video Game Designer	$79,900	19%
3.	Landman	$103,000	13%
4.	Patent Agent	$126,000	13%
5.	Hospital Administrator	$114,000	23%
6.	Continuous Improvement Mgr.	$96,600	12%
7.	Clinical Nurse Specialist	$89,300	19%
8.	Database Developer	$88,200	23%
9.	Info. Assurance Analyst	$96,400	37%
10.	Pilates/Yoga Instructor	$62,400	13%
11.	Clinical Applications Specialist	$84,300	25%
12.	Portfolio Manager	$123,000	27%
13.	Dentist	$152,000	16%
14.	User Experience Designer	$89,300	18%
15.	Auditing Director	$132,000	13%
16.	Real Estate Development Mgr.	$107,000	12%
17.	IT Program Manager	$122,000	15%
18.	Project Control Specialist	$86,600	19%
19.	Pharmacist in Charge	$125,000	15%
20.	QA Coordinator (RN)	$69,300	19%
21.	Strategy Manager	$112,000	19%
22.	Product Development Director	$131,000	12%
23.	Physical Therapy Director	$87,900	23%
24.	Emergency Room Physician	$274,000	19%
25.	Product Analyst	$67,800	32%
26.	Rehabilitation Services Mgr.	$86,900	23%
27.	Health Information Mgt. Dir.	$81,900	23%
28.	Product Mgt. Director	$148,000	13%
29.	Practice Administrator	$78,300	23%
30.	Facilities Director	$97,500	12%
31.	Accounting Director	$103,000	13%
32.	Software QA Manager	$110,000	15%

6,000,000 MINUTES ON THE CLOCK

33.	Orthopedic Surgeon	$410,000	23%
34.	Clinical Services Director	$77,600	23%
35.	Clinical Pharmacist	$117,000	15%
36.	Anesthesiologist	$340,000	24%
37.	Biomedical Engineer	$82,400	27%
38.	IT Security Consultant	$110,000	37%
39.	Telecom. Network Engineer	$90,500	15%
40.	Technical Consultant	$101,000	23%
41.	Customer Service Director	$103,000	12%
42.	Payroll Director	$99,000	12%
43.	Private Banker	$86,500	27%
44.	Operations Director	$108,000	12%
45.	Risk Management Director	$121,000	12%
46.	Construction Manager	$88,700	16%
47.	R & D Engineer, IT	$108,000	20%
48.	Business Development Dir.	$136,000	13%
49.	Proposal Manager	$87,600	13%
50.	Financial Accounting Mgr.	$74,500	13%
51.	Career Services Director	$62,700	12%
52.	Hand Therapist	$83,000	36%
53.	Strategic Planning Director	$139,000	12%
54.	Internal Auditing Manager	$101,000	13%
55.	Consulting Manager	$130,000	19%
56.	Alumni Affairs Director	$64,200	15%
57.	Finance & Administration Mgr.	$74,300	12%
58.	Analytics Manager	$109,000	27%
59.	Nursing Manager	$82,400	23%
60.	Web Analyst	$72,300	25%
61.	Health Care Administrator	$81,000	23%
62.	Business Development Mgr.	$99,600	13%
63.	Regional HR Manager	$84,900	13%
64.	Athletic Director (University)	$70,500	15%
65.	Product Marketing Specialist	$67,600	32%
66.	Implementation Consultant	$91,800	19%
67.	Network Architect	$122,000	15%
68.	Nursing Informatics Analyst	$69,400	25%

6,000,000 MINUTES ON THE CLOCK

69.	Research Analyst	$64,400	32%
70.	Assisted Living Director	$56,400	23%
71.	IT Network Engineer	$79,100	12%
72.	Business Mgr., eCommerce	$82,600	12%
73.	Assoc. Partner, Consulting Svc.	$196,000	19%
74.	Healthcare Consultant	$108,000	13%
75.	Contract Administration Mgr.	$77,400	12%
76.	Regional Property Manager	$80,600	12%
77.	Principal Architect	$132,000	17%
78.	Practice Manager	$63,900	23%
79.	Analytics Director	$142,000	13%
80.	Civil Engineer	$77,400	20%
81.	Lead Physical Therapist	$84,700	36%
82.	Financial Reporting Manager	$96,800	12%
83.	Database Admin. (DBA) Mgr.	$120,000	15%
84.	Marketing Consultant	$90,700	32%
85.	Biostatistician	$98,800	27%
86.	Athletic Coach	$47,000	15%
87.	Financial Analysis Manager	$99,800	16%
88.	Content Strategist	$80,000	32%
89.	Transportation Engineer	$78,100	20%
90.	Information Tech. Auditor	$88,200	25%
91.	Assisted Living Administrator	$55,500	23%
92.	Systems Analyst	$83,800	25%
93.	Tech Support Engineer	$75,400	20%
94.	Public Relations Director	$90,500	13%
95.	Auditing Manager	$90,900	13%
96.	Program Mgt. Dir. Human Svcs.	$55,500	13%
97.	Environ. Health/Safety Dir.	$114,000	15%
98.	Database Administrator	$89,100	15%
99.	Structural Engineer	$80,400	20%
100.	Clinical Lab Supervisor	$66,900	30%

6,000,000 MINUTES ON THE CLOCK

Happiness Index: Top 200 Careers with the Highest Job Satisfaction Ratings

Methodology: The following career ratings represent averages taken from the responses of 13,871 MyPlan.com users during registration in 2014. Users were asked to rate how happy they were in their current occupation by indicating that they were either "Very Happy," "Happy," "Mixed / Neutral," "Not Happy," or "Miserable". The scores below are normalized on a 100-point scale with 0 being "Miserable" and 100 being "Very Happy".

1. Singers	91.7
2. Municipal Fire Fighters	90.0
3. Aircraft Assemblers - Structure, Surfaces, Rigging & System	83.3
4. Pediatricians – General	80.0
5. College Professors – Communications	79.2
6. Educational, Vocational & School Counselors	78.8
7. Managers of Animal Husbandry Animal Care Workers	78.6
8. Criminal Investigators & Special Agents	77.5
9. College Professors – Psychology	76.9
10. College Instructors - Vocational Studies	76.7
11. High School Teachers - Vocational Studies	76.3
12. Coaches & Scouts	75.0
13. College Professors – Business	75.0
14. Veterinary Technologists & Technicians	72.9
15. Chief Executives	72.4
16. Physician Assistants	72.2
17. Supervisors/Managers of Tactical Operations Specialists	71.4
18. Rehabilitation Counselors	70.8
19. Clergy	70.8
20. College Professors - Philosophy & Religion	70.8
21. Private Detectives & Investigators	70.8
22. College Instructors – Education	70.4

6,000,000 MINUTES ON THE CLOCK

23. Self-Enrichment Education Teachers	70.0
24. Middle School Teachers - Vocational Studies	70.0
25. Athletes & Sports Competitors	70.0
26. College Professors – History	70.0
27. Arbitrators, Mediators & Conciliators	70.0
28. Mental Health Counselors	69.0
29. Actors	67.9
30. Commercial & Industrial Designers	67.9
31. Skin Care Specialists	67.5
32. Bus Drivers – School	67.2
33. College Instructors – Medicine & Health Specialties	66.7
34. Managers/Supervisors of Police & Detectives	66.7
35. Chiropractors	66.7
36. Lodging Managers	65.9
37. Physical Therapists	65.8
38. Court Reporters	65.6
39. Operating Engineers/Construction Equipment Operators	65.6
40. Emergency Medical Technicians (EMT) & Paramedics	65.5
41. Financial Examiners	65.4
42. Cost Estimators	65.0
43. Recreation Workers	65.0
44. College Professors – English Language & Literature	64.5
45. Instructional Coordinators	64.4
46. Medical Equipment Preparers	64.3
47. Dispatchers (except police, fire & ambulance)	64.3
48. Tax Preparers	64.3
49. Education Administrators – College	64.1
50. Operations Research Analysts	63.9
51. Photographers	63.9
52. Wholesale & Retail Buyers	63.8
53. Dietitians & Nutritionists	63.6
54. Occupational Therapists	63.6
55. Technical Directors & Production Managers	63.6
56. Correctional Officers & Jailers	63.3
57. Massage Therapists	63.3
58. High School Teachers	63.2

6,000,000 MINUTES ON THE CLOCK

59. Chefs & Head Cooks	63.2
60. Librarians	62.9
61. Mechanical Engineers	62.8
62. Medical & Health Services Managers	62.8
63. Statisticians	62.5
64. Packers & Packagers	62.5
65. Inspectors, Testers, Sorters, Samplers, Weighers	62.5
66. Social Science Research Assistants	62.5
67. Pharmacists	62.5
68. Counseling Psychologists	62.5
69. Dental Hygienists	62.5
70. Copy Writers	62.5
71. Construction Managers	62.5
72. Materials Engineers	62.5
73. Creative Writers — Authors, Poets & Lyricists	61.8
74. Art Directors	61.7
75. Middle School Teachers	61.6
76. Substance Abuse & Behavioral Disorder Counselors	61.6
77. Environmental Scientists & Specialists	61.5
78. Mental Health & Substance Abuse Social Workers	61.5
79. Medical & Public Health Social Workers	61.1
80. Bus Drivers - Transit & Intercity	61.1
81. Managers/Supervisors of Landscaping Workers	61.1
82. Education Administrators — Elementary & High School	60.7
83. General & Operations Managers	60.7
84. Directors - Religious Activities & Education	60.5
85. Computer Operators	60.4
86. Helpers — Installation, Maintenance & Repair Workers	60.0
87. Internists — General	60.0
88. Construction & Building Inspectors	60.0
89. Musicians	60.0
90. Surveyors	60.0
91. Loan Interviewers & Clerks	60.0
92. Radar & Sonar Technicians	60.0
93. Licensed Practical & Licensed Vocational Nurses	60.0
94. Medical & Clinical Laboratory Technicians	59.7

6,000,000 MINUTES ON THE CLOCK

95. Treasurers & Controllers	59.7
96. Medical Records & Health Information Technicians	59.6
97. Electronics Engineers	59.6
98. Producers	59.4
99. Machine Setters, Operators & Tenders - Metal and Plastic	59.4
100. Teaching Assistants	59.0
101. Adult Literacy, Remedial Education & GED Teachers	58.8
102. Hairdressers, Hairstylists & Cosmetologists	58.6
103. Child, Family & School Social Workers	58.5
104. Automotive Master Mechanics	58.3
105. Surgical Technologists	58.3
106. Marriage & Family Therapists	58.3
107. Health Educators	58.3
108. Credit Analysts	58.3
109. Stock Clerks - Stockroom, Warehouse or Storage Yard	58.3
110. Purchasing Agents	58.3
111. Social & Human Service Assistants	58.1
112. Machinists	58.0
113. Engineering Managers	57.9
114. Human Resources Assistants (exc. payroll & timekeeping)	57.9
115. Truck Drivers - Heavy & Tractor-Trailer	57.8
116. Managers of Non-Retail Sales Workers	57.8
117. Interior Designers	57.8
118. Fashion Designers	57.7
119. Property, Real Estate & Community Association Managers	57.4
120. Fine Artists — Painters, Sculptors & Illustrators	57.3
121. Bus & Truck Mechanics and Diesel Engine Specialists	57.1
122. Electronic Drafters	57.1
123. Civil Drafters	57.1
124. Special Forces	57.1
125. Public Relations Managers	57.1
126. Computer & Information Systems Managers	56.8
127. Welders, Cutters & Welder Fitters	56.8
128. Architects	56.5
129. Administrative Services Managers	56.5
130. Sales Managers	56.3

6,000,000 MINUTES ON THE CLOCK

131. Managers/Supervisors of Agricultural Workers   56.3
132. Mechanical Drafters   56.3
133. Airfield Operations Specialists   56.3
134. Aerospace Engineers   56.3
135. Managers/Supervisors of Construction/Extraction Workers   56.1
136. Construction Carpenters   56.1
137. Management Analysts   55.9
138. Family & General Practitioners   55.8
139. Storage & Distribution Managers   55.8
140. Social & Community Service Managers   55.7
141. Airline Pilots, Copilots & Flight Engineers   55.6
142. Electrical Repairers — Commercial & Industrial Equipment   55.6
143. Payroll & Timekeeping Clerks   55.4
144. Editors   55.4
145. Managers of Mechanics, Installers & Repairers   55.4
146. Nuclear Medicine Technologists   55.0
147. Occupational Health & Safety Specialists   55.0
148. Plumbers   55.0
149. Industrial Production Managers   55.0
150. Graphic Designers   55.0
151. Electrical & Electronic Equipment Assemblers   55.0
152. Merchandise Displayers & Window Trimmers   55.0
153. Maintenance Workers — Machinery   55.0
154. College Professors — Engineering   55.0
155. Medical Assistants   54.7
156. Elementary School Teachers   54.7
157. Pharmacy Technicians   54.7
158. Financial Managers, Branch or Department   54.6
159. Sales Engineers   54.4
160. Cooks — Restaurant   54.3
161. Construction Laborers   54.3
162. Marketing Managers   54.3
163. Opticians — Dispensing   54.2
164. Film & Video Editors   54.2
165. Preschool Teachers   54.0
166. Public Relations Specialists   53.8

6,000,000 MINUTES ON THE CLOCK

167. Managers of Production & Operating Workers	53.8
168. Sales Representatives — Wholesale & Manufacturing	53.7
169. Police Patrol Officers	53.6
170. Structural Metal Fabricators & Fitters	53.6
171. Radio & Television Announcers	53.6
172. Speech-Language Pathologists	53.3
173. Helpers - Production Workers	53.2
174. Manicurists & Pedicurists	53.1
175. Sales Representatives — Technical & Scientific Products	53.0
176. Computer, Automated Teller & Office Machine Repairers	52.8
177. Eligibility Interviewers - Government Programs	52.8
178. Landscaping & Groundskeeping Workers	52.8
179. Fitness Trainers & Aerobics Instructors	52.8
180. Medical & Clinical Laboratory Technologists	52.8
181. Veterinarians	52.8
182. Accountants	52.7
183. Food Service Managers	52.1
184. Aircraft Mechanics & Service Technicians	52.1
185. Claims Examiners — Property & Casualty Insurance	52.1
186. Security Guards	52.1
187. Bill & Account Collectors	51.9
188. Hosts & Hostesses — Restaurant, Lounge & Coffee Shop	51.7
189. Dancers	51.7
190. Personal Financial Advisors	51.5
191. Managers/Supervisors of Office & Administrative Workers	51.4
192. Bookkeeping, Accounting & Auditing Clerks	51.3
193. Concierges	51.3
194. Managers of Food Preparation & Serving Workers	51.1
195. Loan Officers & Mortgage Brokers	51.0
196. Purchasing Managers	51.0
197. Civil Engineers	50.9
198. Personal & Home Care Aides	50.6
199. Painters - Construction & Maintenance	50.0
200. Pharmacy Aides	50.0

6,000,000 MINUTES ON THE CLOCK

Forbes Ten Happiest Jobs – 2011
1. Clergy
2. Firefighters
3. Physical Therapists
4. Authors
5. Special Education Teachers
6. Teachers
7. Artists
8. Psychologists
9. Financial Services Sales Agents
10. Operating engineers

Forbes Ten Happiest Jobs – 2015
1. School Principal
2. Executive Chef
3. Loan Officer
4. Automation Engineer
5. Research Assistant
6. Database Administrator
7. Website Developer
8. Business Development Executive
9. Senior Software Engineer
10. Systems Developer

Forbes Ten Most Hated Jobs – 2011
1. Director of Information Technology
2. Director of Sales and Marketing
3. Product Manager
4. Senior Web Developer
5. Technical Specialist
6. Electronics Technician
7. Law Clerk
8. Technical Support Analyst
9. CNC Machinist
10. Marketing Manager

6,000,000 MINUTES ON THE CLOCK

Forbes Ten Most Hated Jobs – 2015
1. Security Guard
2. Merchandiser
3. Salesperson
4. Dispatcher
5. Clerk
6. Research Analyst
7. Legal Assistant
8. Technical Support Agent
9. Truck Driver
10. Customer Service Specialist

As you review these listings, you may notice inconsistencies. Jobs may be ranked high on one list and low on another. The list of happiest and unhappiest jobs had an almost complete turnover in just four years. Jobs that people default into because they don't have better options aren't likely to have a high ranking. Because you're a unique individual, you could probably find a job in the bottom ten of a list and rank it higher personally than a job in the top ten of a list. Rankings like these may be more useful as a guide to jobs you want to avoid rather than jobs you want to pursue.

You will need to research the position you are seeking to know what the salary range is for that position. You also want to know the employer's situation. You are looking for information on how urgent it is for them to fill this position, the quantity and quality of the competition, and who is in the position to offer you the job and its salary without someone else's approval.

If it can be arranged, it is best to have two meetings – one to clarify the job responsibilities, and a second meeting to discuss the compensation package. Because of the importance of both topics, you want to come across as thorough and thoughtful.

Do not accept a job offer without sleeping on it. Even if the offer is beyond your wildest expectations, it's not going anywhere overnight. If they want you today, they'll still want you tomorrow. You need that time away from them to process the offer and to see if there is room to negotiate. (There usually is.)

When contemplating how high they might go, you can be sure that they won't pay you more than what your new boss makes, so you know your ceiling is somewhere below that figure. How much below may be hard to tell. If you state your minimum salary just below their maximum salary, you can negotiate and still end up at the high end of the salary range for that position.

There is an additional advantage in having gone over all the job responsibilities prior to negotiating salary. In order to get a higher salary than they are offering, you may want to see what additional responsibilities you are in a position to accept. It is important to approach this and every negotiation from a win-win perspective. If the company feels like they are getting a top-flight employee with an eagerness to assume responsibility, they shouldn't mind paying a competitive salary for such a person.

One more thing – companies will want to know your salary history. It is not in your interest to provide that information. If your current salary is considerably lower than what this new job typically pays, the company may try to low-ball you on salary. If you are making a career change that involves less pay, the company may be concerned you can't make the adjustment, and will soon leave for more money. If they press you, politely but firmly point out:

6,000,000 MINUTES ON THE CLOCK

- The old salary was for the old job. The new salary is for the new job. It's apples and oranges.
- Their benchmark is what other prospective employers will pay. That's their competition, not your old job.
- You've researched this position; you know what the salary range is, and it's not a problem for you.

6,000,000 MINUTES ON THE CLOCK

WHAT ARE THEY SAYING ABOUT YOU?

Three seconds. One-one-thousand, two-one-thousand, three-one-thousand. That's it. That's how much time it takes to evaluate you.

Of course, someone as complex as you cannot be evaluated in a mere three seconds. Nevertheless, in that brief period, people who are in a position to offer you the job of your dreams, to forever change your life for the better, may blow you off because your jewelry is tacky.

It's not fair, but we all do it. We have so many potential interactions with people in a typical day that we have to set up screening mechanisms to protect ourselves. Someone who conducts interviews for a corporation sees hundreds, if not thousands of job applicants a year. More than most, these people need quick methods to carve the unqualified applicants from the herd.

In those first three seconds, you will be scoped out from head to toe. Your grooming, demeanor, mannerisms, and body language will all be evaluated. If you appear to match the corporate culture, you'll still be in contention.

You have to make several first impressions. The assistant of the person interviewing you will have a first impression, and the interviewer will want to know about it. Blow it with the assistant, and you might as well go home. Every person you meet will each have a first impression, and they will talk to each other; what you show them better be consistent. The worst impression any of them have may become the dominant one. This is a screening process, after all. You may even be scrutinized via security cameras while you wait in the reception area or walk to the next interview. You're under a microscope the minute you set foot on their turf.

If you're young and just starting your working life, you will quickly learn that in the adult world, "popular" doesn't exist. No one was ever voted most popular at any Fortune 500 company. **Popularity is replaced in the working world by** *competence.* Competence means being able to do your job to at least the minimum level of expectations. The root word of competent is *compete*, and to be competent means you are able to compete with others who are doing the same thing.

Competence breeds confidence. If you want to be self-confident in your work, you must first become competent in your work. If you want others to be confident in your work, they must be able to see evidence of your competence in your work. Regardless of how popular you may have been in high school, it won't mean a thing in the workplace if you can't be counted on to do your job.

Your Life On a Page

To get to the interview, you must first survive the initial screening of your cover letter and résumé. You aren't writing a résumé for you – you are writing it for the readers. Put yourself in the readers' shoes – they look at dozens of résumés every day, and they are looking for something to disqualify it quickly.

First rule: No Typos! A résumé with spelling, grammar, or punctuation errors is totally unacceptable. You have word processors, spell check, and all kinds of software to help you. Also, always proof a paper copy of anything you send out; don't just proof what's on the computer screen. There are often errors we only catch when we see it on paper.

If you send a résumé with errors, it will end up in the trash, regardless of your qualifications. The reader will assume such carelessness is typical of your work and will automatically disqualify you from further consideration.

Because résumés tend to be scanned rather than read, it should be no more than one page. **Edit ruthlessly.** Tweak your résumé for each reader. That doesn't mean major rewrites, but different employers are looking for different characteristics. Since you will have researched any company you send a résumé to, you should have an idea what they value most and what they are looking for in a new hire. Something as simple as setting key words in bold type so they stand out can cause your résumé to be read, rather than merely scanned.

Don't put personal information (age, religion, hobbies, etc.) on your résumé. Education, work experience, skill sets, and **what you offer them** are what need to be on there.

One last most important rule about your résumé – **Never lie**. If the lie is caught before you're hired, you won't be. If it's caught after you're hired, you'll be fired. Lies are easy to catch because so much of your history is available, often just by going online. And even if you're never caught, you're still doomed to fail. No relationship built on a lie ever succeeds.

Sartorial Perfection

"You're wearing that?!" This criticism-as-question is bad enough on Saturday night, but it's the last thing you

6,000,000 MINUTES ON THE CLOCK

should hear when dressing for a job interview. When selecting your ensemble for any business meeting, but especially for a job interview, remember the old medical dictum, "First, do no harm."

There is an old adage that you don't dress for the job you have, but for the job you want. **If you don't look the part, you aren't likely to get the part.** The first thing to find out is what the prescribed attire is for your desired position in that particular company. Because companies can vary widely on what they consider appropriate dress, you may see accountants in one company in three-piece suits and their counterparts in another company in jeans. It's up to you to find out the dress code before the interview. Ask someone in their Human Resources department if you're not sure. It is also better to err on the side of being overdressed if there's any doubt about what's appropriate to wear.

Make sure your clothing is clean, spot-free, and pressed. Don't wear anything with frayed cuffs or collars. Understated colors and patterns are best. Make sure that everything you put on is coordinated. The goal is to have the interviewer notice only you, not your clothing. You don't want to compete for the interviewer's attention with your own ensemble.

For everyone, but especially women, do not wear anything that could be considered sexually provocative, unless sex is part of the job description. An outfit that might be attractive in a social setting can be very distractive in a business setting. Know the difference.

Be the epitome of hygiene. Bathe or shower before you go. Use deodorant. Brush your teeth and use mouthwash. Shave. Tame your hair. Unkempt may be the style, but you don't want to give anyone the chance to associate the word sloppy with you. Make-up should be applied with the idea of hiding flaws, rather than enhancing beauty. And nix the perfume and cologne. At best, it's another distraction. At worst, the interviewer could be allergic, ending the interview before it begins.

Lastly, no visible tattoos or body piercings, unless you're certain the interviewer has them, too. The higher up you go in the interview process, the older and more conservative the interviewer tends to be. Freedom of expression is fine, but you don't want to express yourself right out of contention.

The Unsaid

One of the reasons that people are evaluating you before you are even introduced is that 80-90% of our communication is non-verbal. Some key areas of non-verbal communication are:

- **Promptness** – Like Shakespeare said, better three hours too soon than one minute too late. Nothing short of Armageddon is an acceptable excuse. **Get your ass there on time!**
- **Eye Contact** – Failure to make eye contact indicates you are weak, submissive, and dishonest. You may be none of those things, but that's the message you send when you don't look them in the eye. If making eye contact is difficult, look at their nose or mouth. Unless their face is within a foot of yours, they can't tell the difference.
- **The Handshake** – The proper grip is somewhere between dead fish and pro wrestler. Three pumps and release. One hand only unless you're consoling someone. Also, maintain eye contact when shaking hands.
- **Your Face** – Who doesn't love a smiling face? It

indicates warmth, friendliness, and most important in an interview, affiliation. (Don't worry; your teeth look just fine.) Besides, a smile begins with the eyes, which is why eye contact is important. You smile with your eyes - your mouth just goes along for the ride.
- **Posture** – Erect (but not rigid) posture indicates strength, health, and self-confidence. Head up, shoulders back. Lean forward slightly when sitting to indicate you are attentive and interested in what the other person is saying.
- **Proximity and Touching** – In American culture, our personal space is about two feet in all directions. In formal situations like a job interview, everyone should respect everyone else's personal space, which is one reason not to wear provocative clothing or scents for an interview. It can be perceived as an invitation into your personal space, which one doesn't do in a business environment.
- **Gestures** – Because we are naturally nervous in an interview situation, there is a greater tendency to rock, tap feet, twitch, and gesture with our hands more than usual. Even if you're a bundle of nerves inside, you want to give the impression of quiet self-confidence and serenity. Proper posture helps, as does taking regular deep breaths to relax you. Try not to have anything in your hands during the interview (it promotes fidgeting). Keep your hands folded in your lap as much as possible. Occasional hand gestures are fine; just try not to look like a marionette on meth when you're making them.
- **Gum** – Don't even think about it.

6,000,000 MINUTES ON THE CLOCK

"I've told you why I need a dog. Now suppose you tell me what makes you think you might be that dog."

The Said

At this point, you have managed to run the gauntlet of screenings to enable you to sit down and actually have an interview. The first thing to recognize is the difference between an interview and an interrogation. In an interview, the interviewer is gathering information that the interviewee (you) generally wants the interviewer to have. In an interrogation, the interviewer is trying to extract information that the interviewee wants to keep hidden. An interrogation is an adversarial relationship. An interview should be a mutually beneficial one, which is why being truthful about everything prior to the interview is so important. **You want to keep the interview from becoming an interrogation.**

The prefix *inter* means between or among. In an interview, both parties should be gaining a better *view* of each other, which means **you should be asking questions as well.** Asking questions is a sign of interest and intelligence. Research the company and the position you're seeking before the interview. The information you gather should generate some questions. Your research will also help you generate more substantive questions, demonstrating your diligence. Have your questions written down so you can remember to ask all of them, which will also show you're organized.

Two bits of advice, though. First, don't attempt to take control of the interview. Wait until the topic is on one of your questions before asking it. You may need to wait until the end of the interview to ask many of your questions. You should always be given the opportunity to ask questions before the interview concludes. Second, ask your questions in a manner that doesn't put the other person on the defensive. If you can ask a question in terms of seeking clarification or illumination on a topic, it is less likely to be viewed as confrontational.

Just as the nervousness of the situation can make us more fidgety, nerves cause us to answer too quickly and to speak at too fast a pace. **Before answering any question, take a breath.** That three second pause indicates you are giving thought to the question, not just blurting out anything. It's amazing the dumb things we *don't* say if we give ourselves three seconds to run it through our brain before it comes out of our mouth. If they ask you twenty questions in the interview, all of these pauses will add one additional minute to the interview - time well spent.

Taking a few seconds to collect our thoughts also cuts down the use of fillers – *you know, like, umm, dude*, etc. You must be conscious of your use of these phrases and make a conscious effort to eliminate them from your speech. The habit of using them usually develops in the teen years. You don't want the interviewer to think your communication skills haven't improved since tenth grade.

Slower speech is clearer speech. Proper enunciation makes your words easier to understand. If you are asked more than once to repeat something because they couldn't understand you, you've got a problem. Making the conscious effort to slow down your speech may make it sound agonizingly slow to your ear. However, to the person you are trying to impress, it sounds just right.

An accent is anything that doesn't sound like you. Accents, regional and foreign, may require special attention. It takes time to modify a strong accent. Pacing is very important in these situations. A fast speaking pace, combined with an unfamiliar accent will be very hard to understand. Be aware if people are having a problem understanding you because of your accent. Slowing down and enunciating can overcome a lot of the problem.

It's getting harder and harder to find proper grammar in popular culture. Remember your high school language arts classes? If you paid attention in those classes, the interview is the payoff. If your grammar is on the atrocious side, keep your answers short and simple to make it less obvious. You may also consider only jobs where communication skills are not a high priority.

A Class Act

Everyone has at his/her disposal what is arguably the single most effective tool to get people to like you and want you on their team. Strangely enough, relatively few people bother to use this tool. I'm referring to good manners.

The importance of good manners on a macro scale is best stated in the book *How Good People Make Tough Choices:*

"Three great domains of human action are positive law, free choice, and manners. Manners operate in the domain between positive law and absolute freedom. It is the domain of obedience to the unenforceable. We enforce the law upon ourselves. This ethical middle ground is constantly at risk of encroachment from both sides.

When ethics collapses, law rushes in to fill the void. Regulation is necessary to sustain human interaction. Certain behaviors must be followed, if not voluntarily, then by compulsion."

Good manners on a micro scale are not about which fork to use at dinner. Good manners are about something simpler, yet more difficult to follow: The Golden Rule – Do unto others as you would have them do unto you.

Good manners are based on the axiom that first you give, then you get. If you treat people with consideration first, you can expect consideration in return. If you give someone consideration, but don't receive it in return, that should tell you something about the other person's character and whether you would want to work with him/her.

Good manners require you to be other-centered, rather than self-centered. Before you speak or act, you think about how your words or actions will be received by others. You consider their feelings and sensibilities. If you think your words or actions might offend someone, you make a determination whether the situation warrants

6,000,000 MINUTES ON THE CLOCK

such behavior. Feeling better at someone else's expense is not only not a justification, it's bad manners. Even when the other party is guilty of bad manners or worse, there is no need to sink to their level. **High principles and good manners are not mutually exclusive.**

As a practical demonstration of your good manners, it is imperative that you **send a hand-written Thank You note to everyone with whom you interview.** An e-mail is not sufficient for something this important. An e-mail takes almost no effort and gets lost among the dozens of e-mails your interviewer gets every day. It takes five minutes to hand write a three sentence Thank You note and address the envelope. (Get the interviewer's business card so you have the address.) You will be amazed at how such a small effort on your part can help you get what you want. If 90% of the interviewees don't bother to send a Thank You note, but you do, you've just given yourself an edge over 90% of the competition. What other five minute task gives you that kind of competitive advantage?

Face Time

Technology can be wonderful for keeping in touch with people who are at a distance, but technology has also caused interference with the ability and desire to communicate face to face. We seem all too eager to let electronic communication supersede good old-fashioned conversation.

There is no communication involving technology that will ever be better than face-to-face communication. Webinars have a place, but the more important the meeting, the less appropriate they are. If there is bad news to be delivered, it is always better (though harder for the messenger) to tell the affected people in person, rather than informing them electronically. The 2009 movie *Up In the Air* explored the delicate process of telling people they are losing their jobs. An unsuccessful attempt to perform this task via computer screens in the film illustrated the intangible benefits of face-to-face communication.

Networking is still the best way to land a good job in the right field. But make no mistake – networking is a face-to-face process. LinkedIn, Facebook, chat rooms, and any other electronic social media are not true networking. Networking involves meeting with people, pressing the flesh, schmoozing, shaking hands, patting backs, smiling, gesturing, and all the hundreds of other ways humans communicate with each other using more than typed words. Even the telephone at least enables the other person to hear your voice inflections, which can communicate more than a text message. Even a telephone call isn't as good as face time because you cannot see or touch the other person. **The more of your senses that can be involved with the communication, the more effective that communication will be.**

If you are looking for leads in all the traditional places, you aren't likely to turn up anything but leftovers from all the others who have been picking over the same territory. **The best first contacts in a job search are the people who know you best**, and these people are also the people you see the most on a face to face basis. You may not think these close contacts have other contacts of their own, but you'd be surprised how quickly such a network spreads out. Also, because these people know you and like you, they are more likely to expend some serious effort on your behalf to connect you with someone who can get you that ideal job.

6,000,000 MINUTES ON THE CLOCK

Some of the best sources for help in your job search are people you have worked with on some altruistic level. These are people you work with at a place of worship, a Rotary Club or other civic organization, or any activity where you have involved yourself for the benefit of others. Your contacts there have seen you at your best, and they are likely to have contacts that can help you. More important, they are likely to want to help you because they have seen you helping others.

Whenever you have the opportunity to spend time with people face to face, take advantage of it. Never forego an opportunity to communicate with someone who is in your presence to communicate with someone who is not in your presence. The quality of face to face communication cannot be matched by *any* electronic device, now or ever.

What's Out There on You?

You've almost made it. You survived all the screening processes. You had a great interview, following the advice laid out here, and now you're waiting for the call saying they want to hire you.

Your potential employer has another step to take first. They will call and confirm prior employment history, and they may call some of your references, which is no problem because you've been totally honest about everything.

They will also check you out on Google, Intelius, Facebook, Instagram, Snapchat, and any other website that might have information about you.

There are two groups of sites they will look at, so you need to look at them first. Check out information about you that has been generated by others. Websites like

6,000,000 MINUTES ON THE CLOCK

Intelius can list any criminal record. Any organization to which you belong (or belonged) may have information about you on their website. Google yourself to see what is out there that others can learn about you. If there is incorrect information about you out there, contact the website in question and request they correct or delete the information. If there is incorrect potentially harmful information out there, you may need to be pre-emptive and let your potential employer know about it up front. Making them aware of it and documenting the errors may save some awkward questions later and will make you look like you're on top of everything.

Nothing on any of those sites may be as harmful as what you may have put out there yourself. Websites like Facebook are not targeted to potential employers, but potential employers are looking at them to learn more about job candidates. Many people aren't getting hired because of what is posted out there.

Frank revelations (often with pictures) about drugs, sex, drinking, and other improprieties will not commend you to any employer. Even if some of the claims are merely posturing to impress peers, it won't make any difference. At the very least, it would demonstrate extremely poor judgment on your part. An employer would also be concerned that co-workers, customers, and competitors might see it, hurting you and your employer.

If there's anything out there about you on any personal website, and if you aren't willing to print it out and submit it along with your résumé, then you need to shut it down. The issue isn't about freedom of expression; it's about not shooting yourself in the foot when opportunity knocks. If you want to work with mature adults, you have to prove you are one of them.

There is something else that almost all potential

employers will look at, and you might not even think they would bother. **Part of the background check for job applicants now includes obtaining a copy of the applicant's credit report.** Since the employer is paying you, rather than being paid by you, wanting to see your credit report doesn't seem to make sense. However, there are actually some good reasons for employers to check out this part of your life.

While it's true that the employee runs a financial risk if the employer has financial problems, those risks are generally limited to pay earned, but not yet received. The employer runs a much greater risk if the employee has financial problems. Theft from the employer is the most common risk. Theft may entail stealing property from the employer. The greater risk is the theft of money from the employer, primarily through fraud. This risk is high because one can often steal funds from the company electronically, which is harder to catch than someone loading merchandise into the trunk of a car. Also, theft from fraud can go on for years, and its detection may only come after thousands of dollars have been stolen and spent.

An employee with financial problems also presents the risk of a frivolous lawsuit against the employer. The employee overburdened with debt is more likely to look for a lawsuit, any lawsuit, to provide a quick cash settlement and a way out of debt. Even if the lawsuit is baseless, the cost of defending a lawsuit gives the employee hope that the employer might settle out of court.

Finally, your credit report can give the potential employer (who hardly knows you at this point) some insight into how you manage your affairs. If your credit report indicates that your management of your personal business affairs is a disaster, they will not be confident that your management of their business affairs will be any better. Even if there is no chance for you to steal from the company, mismanagement of your own money is a huge strike against you when competing against others for a plum job. Next to a shining (and accurate) résumé, a shining credit report is one of the best arrows to have in your quiver when you're hunting down a new job.

Fingernails on a Blackboard

The annals of TV history are full of them – the irritating co-worker. You have Dwight Schrute from *The Office*, Mimi Bobek from *The Drew Carey Show,* and Ted Baxter from *The Mary Tyler Moore Show,* to name a few. We find them funny for two reasons. First, we don't have to work with them. Second, they either don't know or don't care that they are such a drain and strain on their co-workers.

We've all known people like these at work. What we may almost never know is, are we one of those fingernails-on-a-blackboard personalities? It is unlikely you have been blunt enough to disclose their defects to such a person in your office. Is it possible you are such a person, and no one has yet been blunt enough to point it out to you? You don't want to find all this out at your exit interview, after you finally made the case for them to can you.

An irritating manner or personality may not be enough to get someone fired on its own, but it can serve as incentive to get the employer digging for something less subjective as grounds for termination.

Here are just a few of the many ways you can sour

the office environment and make yourself a target for termination:
- Having loud telephone conversations
- Not cleaning up after yourself in the staff kitchen
- Showing up late for work or for meetings
- Looking at a co-worker's computer screen over his or her shoulder
- Taking supplies from a co-worker's desk
- Neglecting to say please and thank you
- Wearing too much perfume or cologne
- Chewing gum (or anything else) loudly
- Taking the last of something without replacing it
- Talking behind someone's back
- Asking someone to lie for you
- Blaming someone else when you are at fault
- Taking credit for someone else's work
- Asking a subordinate to do something unrelated to work, i.e. run errands
- Trying to convert others to your political or religious beliefs
- Opening someone else's mail
- Sending unwanted email
- Telling offensive jokes
- Smoking in common areas
- Not pulling your own weight
- Complaining about the company, boss, or co-workers
- Having a condescending attitude toward others
- Maintaining a sloppy, unsanitary work area
- Conducting a side business at your main job
- Being under the influence of anything at work
- Gossiping, especially about bosses or co-workers
- Sexual impropriety (by their definition, not yours)
- Discussing personal problems during business hours

6,000,000 MINUTES ON THE CLOCK

Individually, none of these actions would likely get an otherwise competent employee fired. But an accumulation of them, especially in combination with other more serious offenses, almost certainly will. If nothing else, such activities are a drain on co-workers' productivity and morale That's not something a good employer will tolerate for long.

Condemned by Your Own Hard Drive

If your employer is looking for solid cause to terminate you, they can probably find the smoking gun on your office computer.

Take email. Not only is there a log of how much company time you spend on email, there are the emails themselves. Emails of a personal nature are a misuse of company time. Emails that speak negatively about your boss, co-workers, or the company are real trouble. Gossip used to center around the water cooler; now it flies around via email. Before sending any email, either from the company computer or about your company from any computer, ask yourself if you would send that email if you had to copy your boss on it. If you wouldn't want your boss to see it, don't send the email; it'll come back to haunt you.

Emails are not the only thing on your hard drive. There is also a complete record of your downloads – every site and how much company time you wasted there. You may be able to explain going to Amazon to order a birthday gift for your nephew. You won't be able to explain away even one minute spent on a porn site.

What you say about your company and co-workers away from the job can get you fired, too. Many people post work-related entries on personal blogs. Even if it is a personal blog, access to it is still unlimited. Any confidential information about the company or an employee that ends up on a blog is cause for dismissal.

Think of blogging as a public speaking engagement where you have no idea who might be in the audience and every word is recorded. That thought might keep you from blurting out something that will cost you your job. One last thing – never drink and blog.

Even the most obtuse of employees must have some inkling that they might have crossed the line when they performed the deeds that caused the axe to fall. The last thing you want to have happen in your career is to lose your job over something that, in retrospect, all you can say is "What was I thinking?!"

Resume' or Eulogy?

When the wealthiest man in town passed away after a long life, the citizens gathered for the requisite memorial service. Two old friends who had known the deceased for many years were talking. One asked the other, "Do you have any idea how much he left?" The other gentleman replied, "I know exactly. He left it all."

What makes for an outstanding resume' generally makes for a second-rate eulogy. It's ironic. We expend so much effort creating an impressive resume'. Once we're gone, what's on that resume' isn't what people remember about us.

On your resume', you get the opportunity to highlight your personality type, your temperament, and your conative (doing) strengths to your advantage. And you should. But a resume' doesn't lend itself to highlighting your character strengths. If you attempt to highlight the six virtues that Seligman and Peterson studied (wisdom, courage, humanity, justice, temperance, transcendence), you may come across as egotistical. These virtues must be inferred by the reader of your resume'.

It's another irony that the traits of yours that must be only implied on your resume' are actually the traits that employers are really seeking. Smart employers know that skills can be taught, but that virtues are instilled. They also know if they haven't been instilled in you by the time you send them your resume', they can't make the effort to instill them in you.

In his book, *The Road to Character*, David Brooks refers to the part of us that focuses on our resume' as Adam I and the part that focuses on our eulogy as Adam II. He makes these observations:

- Adam I wants to conquer the world.
- Adam II wants to obey a calling to serve the world.
- Adam I asks how things work.
- Adam II asks why things work.
- Adam I wants to venture forth.
- Adam II wants to return to his roots.
- Adam I achieves success by winning victories over others.
- Adam II builds character by winning victories over himself.
- Adam II lives by an inverse logic. You have to give to receive. You have to conquer your desire to get what you crave. Success leads to the greatest failure, which is pride. Failure leads to the greatest success, which is humility and learning.

Brooks also notes that our culture teaches us to promote ourselves and to master skills for success, but doesn't encourage us to learn humility, sympathy, and self-confrontation, which are necessary to build character. A vocation is not found by looking inside and finding your passion. It is found by looking outside and asking what life is asking of us. Working on your career builds a resume'; working on a calling builds a eulogy.

One of the most important books of the 20th Century was *Man's Search for Meaning*, by Viktor Frankl. Frankl was an up-and-coming psychiatrist in Vienna in the late 1930s. He was also Jewish, and his punishment for being Jewish was to be sent to Auschwitz and later Dachau concentration camps. Viktor Frankl's wife, mother, and brother died in the concentration camps – he and his sister were the only family members to survive the Holocaust.

Man's Search for Meaning offers two important perspectives. It serves as a journal and recollection of the daily life in the concentration camps from the perspective of a trained psychologist. It also offers insight into what is most important in life, which too often only becomes clear after great loss.

Here are some of Frankl's perspectives on what we should really want in life:
- Life is not a quest for pleasure or power, but a quest for meaning.
- There are three possible sources for meaning: in work, in love, and in courage during difficult times.
- The way in which a man accepts his fate and all the suffering it entails gives him ample opportunity – even under the most difficult circumstances – to add a deeper meaning to his life.
- Suffering ceases to be suffering at the moment it finds a meaning, such as the meaning of a sacrifice.
- Pleasure is, and must remain, a side-effect or byproduct, and is destroyed and spoiled to the degree to which it is made a goal in itself.

6,000,000 MINUTES ON THE CLOCK

- It did not really matter what we expected from life, but rather what life expected from us. Our answer must consist, not in talk and meditation, but in right action and in right conduct.
- Woe to him who, when the day of his dreams finally came, found it so different from all he had longed for.
- Sometimes the frustrated will to meaning is vicariously compensated for by a will to power, including the most primitive form of the will to power, the will to money.
- A human being is not one in pursuit of happiness, but rather in search of a reason to become happy.

Exactly two months before he was assassinated, Dr. Martin Luther King, Jr. gave a sermon that became known as "The Drum Major Instinct". It was a prophetic sermon. It also serves as a great lesson on how we should think about the mark we want to leave on this world. Here is the conclusion to that sermon:

"Every now and then I guess we all think realistically about that day when we will be victimized with what is life's final common denominator—that something that we call death. We all think about it. And every now and then I think about my own death and I think about my own funeral. And I don't think of it in a morbid sense. And every now and then I ask myself, "What is it that I would want said?" And I leave the word to you this morning.

If any of you are around when I have to meet my day, I don't want a long funeral. And if you get somebody to deliver the eulogy, tell them not to talk too long. And every now and then I wonder what I want them to say. Tell them not to mention that I have

6,000,000 MINUTES ON THE CLOCK

a Nobel Peace Prize—that isn't important. Tell them not to mention that I have three or four hundred other awards—that's not important. Tell them not to mention where I went to school.

I'd like somebody to mention that day that Martin Luther King, Jr., tried to give his life serving others.

I'd like for somebody to say that day that Martin Luther King, Jr., tried to love somebody.

I want you to say that day that I tried to be right on the war question.

I want you to be able to say that day that I did try to feed the hungry.

And I want you to be able to say that day that I did try in my life to clothe those who were naked.

I want you to say on that day that I did try in my life to visit those who were in prison.

I want you to say that I tried to love and serve humanity.

Yes, if you want to say that I was a drum major, say that I was a drum major for justice. Say that I was a drum major for peace. I was a drum major for righteousness. And all of the other shallow things will not matter. I won't have any money to leave behind. I won't have the fine and luxurious things of life to leave behind. But I just want to leave a committed life behind. And that's all I want to say.

If I can help somebody as I pass along,
If I can cheer somebody with a word or song,
If I can show somebody he's traveling wrong,
Then my living will not be in vain.
If I can do my duty as a Christian ought,
If I can bring salvation to a world once wrought,
If I can spread the message as the master taught,
Then my living will not be in vain.

6,000,000 MINUTES ON THE CLOCK

When it's time for your memorial service, no one is going to praise you for your impressive resume' or your wealth accumulation. They will hopefully praise you for your contributions to a better world, for which you may have been rewarded with material comfort. However, no one sucks up to the deceased, rich or not.

You are going to live a long, full productive life. People will be lined up to say good things about you at the end of that long, full productive life. What do you want them to say?

Think about the different groups of people you will come close to in your life. Start with family members. What would you want your siblings to say about you? More important, what would you want your children to say about you? What do you want your professional colleagues to say about you? Think about your professional qualities, your work ethic, and your contributions to your profession.

What will your friends say? Not at the podium, but in small groups after the others have gone. What they say then is the real measure of what they thought of you and your impact on their lives.

What about those other people who don't necessarily fall into one of the above categories? These people could be from your church, your Rotary Club, your hobby group, or any other service or social organization which included you.

What would you want all these people to say about you? What accomplishments would you like them to be able to list? More important, what personal character traits of yours would you want them to be able to testify by examples from your own life? Would there be consistency in their perceptions of you?

Once you have thought of the things you would like

6,000,000 MINUTES ON THE CLOCK

people to say at your funeral, think about the work you must do between now and then to make those words ring true. Then get to work.

If You Don't Remember Anything Else…

- Lifelong learning and adaptability will be required for all the good jobs in the future.
- Your right brain, the creative, crazy half, will be your most important tool.
- A passion for what you do is absolutely vital to both success and happiness at work.
- You are likely to have a far longer lifespan than most, if not all of the companies you will work for.
- Need vs. Want = Require vs. Desire. Know the difference.
- Increased ability to change jobs also means less job security.
- The job should be changed to fit you; you don't change to fit the job.
- Tests like Myers-Briggs can be very useful in assessing what kind of work might be a good fit.
- Tests like Myers-Briggs don't have all the answers.
- Your satisfaction at work is based on factors you select.
- More money won't make you love a job you hate.
- Don't subordinate the mission to the money.
- The money follows the mission.
- If you plan to strike out on your own, be pulled, not pushed into it.
- Some people will let geography determine where they will work. Others prefer to choose who they will work with first and let that choice determine where they will live. To each his/her own.

6,000,000 MINUTES ON THE CLOCK

- Companies and jobs are global and mobile. Your competition is in the next hemisphere, as well as the next cubicle.
- Risk and reward move in the same direction. A change for greater rewards will likely have greater risks.
- Charge for your output, not your input, which means charging by the project, not by the hour. This method benefits those who produce and punishes those who don't.
- Your risk tolerance determines your reward. Your desired reward does not determine your risk tolerance.
- Status quo bias impedes our ability to make objective comparisons between our current and potential jobs.
- Comparing the pros and cons of different jobs in writing can help clarify the better fit for you.
- As the number of job choices increase arithmetically, the anxiety over making the right decision increases geometrically.
- The best places to work focus on getting the best people in place first and then keeping them there.
- Benefits should be looked at very closely when comparing job offers. Benefits packages can easily offset a lower salary.
- Take your time making a decision to accept a job offer. If they want you today, they'll want you tomorrow.
- *Why* is an essay question, not multiple-choice. It is a question answered with opinions and feelings, not just facts. Thought is a prerequisite to answering *Why*.
- To ask *Why* is not to question the legitimacy of something. It is a search for elaboration, illumination, and confirmation.
- When you compete against others, no one wants to help you. When you compete against yourself,

everyone wants to help you.
- Money is not the cause of our work; it is the effect of our work.
- All legitimate work deserves respect because it provides goods and services to our fellow man, making their lives better.
- The right work is a source of energy, not a consumer of our energy.
- The right work does wonders for our self-esteem.
- Work supports your life, not the other way around.
- We can most help our fellow man, thus ourselves, when we are doing the work for which we are best suited.
- Work is one of the best ways to leave the wood pile higher than you found it.
- You need to work and save so that the senior you can live with the independence and dignity you deserve.
- Work provides one of the best ways to leave a legacy of meaning.
- Don't just work on your resume; work on your eulogy.

6,000,000 MINUTES ON THE CLOCK

6,000,000 MINUTES ON THE CLOCK

WORKING WORDS OF WISDOM

Showing up is 80% of life.
-Woody Allen

Work for your future as if you are going to live forever, for your afterlife as if you are going to die tomorrow.
-Arabian Proverb

Nothing is really work unless you would rather be doing something else.
-James M. Barrie

Initiative is to success what a lighted match is to a candle.
-Orlando Battista

Action without study is fatal. Study without action is futile.
-Mary Beard

When you come to a fork in the road – take it.
-Yogi Berra

If you don't know where you're going, you'll end up somewhere else.
-Yogi Berra

The more men, generally speaking, will do for a dollar when they make it, the more that dollar will do for them when they spend it.
-William J. H. Boetcker

6,000,000 MINUTES ON THE CLOCK

Should we measure you by what you have, or by who you are?
> -John Bogle

What the wise man does at the beginning,
the fool does at the end.
> -Warren Buffett

There are three *i*'s in every cycle:
first the innovator, then the imitator, and finally the idiot.
> -Warren Buffett

There is dignity in work only when it is work freely accepted.
> -Albert Camus

Set me a task in which I can put something of my very self, and it is no longer a task; it is joy; it is art.
> -Bliss Carman

Success is getting what you want.
Happiness is wanting what you get.
> -Dale Carnegie

Every man is the son of his own works.
> -Cervantes

Never stand begging for that which you have the power to earn.
> -Cervantes

He who sacrifices his conscience to ambition burns a picture to obtain the ashes.
> -Chinese Proverb

6,000,000 MINUTES ON THE CLOCK

Courage is the first of human qualities because it is the quality which guarantees all the others.
-Winston Churchill

An optimist sees an opportunity in every calamity;
a pessimist sees a calamity in every opportunity.
-Winston Churchill

If you mean to profit, learn to please.
-Winston Churchill

We make a living by what we get;
we make a life by what we give.
-Winston Churchill

Nothing in life is to be feared. It is only to be understood.
-Marie Curie

Genius is one percent inspiration and ninety-nine percent perspiration.
-Thomas Edison

Imagination is more important than knowledge.
-Albert Einstein

Not everything that can be counted counts.
And not everything that counts can be counted.
-Albert Einstein

The best augury of a man's success in his profession is that he thinks it is the finest in the world.
-George Eliot

6,000,000 MINUTES ON THE CLOCK

It is not half as important to burn the midnight oil as it is to be awake in the daytime.
-E. W. Elmore

Poor men seek meat for their stomachs;
rich men seek stomachs for their meat.
-English Proverb

By the work one knows the workman.
-Jean de la Fontaine

Profit is a byproduct of work; happiness is its chief product.
-Henry Ford

If a man empties his purse into his head, no one can take it from him.
-Benjamin Franklin

The best investment is in the tools of one's own trade.
-Benjamin Franklin

By failing to prepare you are preparing to fail.
-Benjamin Franklin

Work has a greater effect than any other technique of living in the direction of binding the individual more closely to reality; in his work, at least, he is securely attached to a part of reality, the human community.
-Sigmund Freud

Work is love made visible.
-Kahlil Gibran

6,000,000 MINUTES ON THE CLOCK

Success is simple.
Do what's right, the right way, at the right time.
          -Arnold Glasow

Beware of wishing for anything in youth, because you will get it in middle age.
          -Goethe

A clever person commits no minor blunders.
          -Goethe

When you hire people who are smarter than you are, you prove you are smarter than they are.
          -R.H. Grant

All problems become smaller if you don't dodge them but confront them. Touch a thistle timidly and it pricks you; grasp it boldly and its spines crumble.
          -Admiral William F. Halsey

All man's gains are the fruit of venturing.
          -Herodotus

There can be no freedom without freedom to fail.
          -Eric Hoffer

There is no education in the second kick of a mule.
          -Ernest Hollings

The important thing is not so much where we stand, as in what direction we are moving.
          -Oliver Wendell Holmes

6,000,000 MINUTES ON THE CLOCK

Change is not made without inconvenience, even from worse to better.
-Richard Hooker

To escape criticism – do nothing, say nothing, be nothing.
-Elbert Hubbard

We work to become, not to acquire.
-Elbert Hubbard

We must dream of an aristocracy of achievement arising out of a democracy of opportunity.
-Thomas Jefferson

The chains of habit are too weak to be felt until they are too strong to be broken.
-Samuel Johnson

The future is purchased by the present.
-Samuel Johnson

He that never labors may know the pains of idleness, but not the pleasures.
-Samuel Johnson

Don't think of retiring from the world until the world will be sorry that you retire.
-Samuel Johnson

Don't compromise yourself. You're all you've got.
-Janis Joplin

6,000,000 MINUTES ON THE CLOCK

Amateurs hope; professionals work.
-Garson Kanin

Happiness is not attained through self-gratification,
but through fidelity to a worthy purpose.
-Helen Keller

The surest way to be happy is to seek happiness for others.
-Martin Luther King, Jr.

They copied all they could copy,
but they couldn't copy my mind;
And I left them sweatin' and stealin',
a year and a half behind.
-Rudyard Kipling

Unless the job means more than the pay it will never pay more.
-H. Bertram Lewis

What kills a skunk is the publicity it gives itself.
-Abraham Lincoln

The heights by men reached and kept,
Were not attained by sudden flight,
But they, while their companions slept,
Were toiling upward in the night.
-Henry Wadsworth Longfellow

If you would hit the mark, you must aim a little above it.
Every arrow that flies feels the attraction of earth.
-Henry Wadsworth Longfellow

6,000,000 MINUTES ON THE CLOCK

The most effective way to cope with change is to help create it.
-L.W. Lynett

There is no security on this earth; only opportunity.
-General Douglas MacArthur

There are three ingredients in the good life:
learning, earning, and yearning.
-Christopher Morley

Ill-luck is, in nine cases out of ten, the result of taking pleasure first and duty second, instead of duty first and pleasure second.
-Theodore T. Munger

Life is like a game of cards. The hand you are dealt represents Determinism. How you play it is Free Will.
-Jawaharlal Nehru

He who has a Why to live can bear almost any How.
-Friedrich Nietzsche

You never get a second chance to make a good first impression.
-Will Rogers

Even if you're on the right track, you'll get run over if you just sit there.
-Will Rogers

When you cease to make a contribution, you begin to die.
-Eleanor Roosevelt

6,000,000 MINUTES ON THE CLOCK

Far better it is to dare mighty things, to win glorious triumphs, even though checkered by failure, than to take rank with those poor spirits who neither enjoy much nor suffer much, for they live in the gray twilight that knows not victory nor defeat.
-Theodore Roosevelt

To be without some of the things you want
is an indispensable part of happiness.
-Bertrand Russell

A goal without a plan is just a wish.
-Antoine de Saint-Exupery

Failures are divided into two classes – those who thought and never did, and those who did and never thought.
-John Charles Salak

Do not choose to be wrong for the sake of being different.
-Lord Samuel

The only place where success comes before work is a dictionary.
-Vidal Sassoon

Success is not the key to happiness.
Happiness is the key to success.
If you love what you are doing, you will be successful.
-Albert Schweitzer

Why not go out on a limb? Isn't that where the fruit is?
-Frank Scully

6,000,000 MINUTES ON THE CLOCK

It is the mind that makes the body rich.
                              -William Shakespeare

The test of a vocation is the love of the drudgery it involves.
                              -Logan Pearsall Smith

The trouble with the rat race is that even if you win, you're still a rat.
                              -Lily Tomlin

Endeavor so to live that when you die, even the undertaker will be sorry.
                              -Mark Twain

Good manners consist of concealing how much we think of ourselves, and how little we think of the other person.
                              -Mark Twain

It is easier to do a job right than to explain why you didn't.
                              -Martin Van Buren

Hell is the state in which we are barred from receiving what we truly need because of the value we give to what we merely want.
                              -Virgil

The best is the enemy of the good.
                              -Voltaire

Work banishes those three great evils, boredom, vice and poverty.
                              -Voltaire

6,000,000 MINUTES ON THE CLOCK

Everything I did in my life that was worthwhile I caught Hell for.
>-Chief Justice Earl Warren

The world of achievement has always belonged to the optimist.
>-J. Harold Wilkens

Education is not the filling of a pail, but the lighting of a fire.
>-W.B. Yeats

It's better to burn out than to rust.
>-Neil Young

REFERENCES

Baldridge, Letitia; *Letitia Baldridge's New Complete Guide to Executive Manners;* Rawson Associates, 1993

Belsky and Gilovich; *Why Smart People Make Big Money Mistakes*; Simon and Schuster, 1999

Bolles, Richard; *What Color is Your Parachute?;* Ten Speed Press, 2006

Branham, Leigh, *The 7 Hidden Reasons Employees Leave;* AMACOM, 2005

Collins, Jim; *Good to Great;* Harper Collins, 2001

Covey, Stephen; *Seven Habits of Highly Effective People;*
Franklin Covey Co., 1990

Daniels, Aubrey, *Bringing Out the Best in People;* McGraw-Hill, 2001

Fitzhenry, Robert, ed.; *The Harper Book of Quotations;* Harper Perennial, 1993

Frederickson, Barbara L.; *The Value of Positive Emotions*; 2003; *American Scientist*

Friedman, Thomas; *The World is Flat;* Farrar, Straus and Giroux, 2006

Goodman, Ted, ed.; *The Forbes Book of Business Quotations;* Black Dog and Leventhal, 1997

Haidt, Jonathan; *The Happiness Hypothesis*; 2006; Basic Books

6,000,000 MINUTES ON THE CLOCK

Harford, Tim; *Adapt*; 2011; Farrar, Straus and Giroux

Harford, Tim; *The Logic of Life*; 2008; Random House

Heath, Chip & Heath, Dan; *Switch*; 2011; Broadway Books

Heathfield, Susan, *The Awesome Power of Goal Setting;* Heathfield Consulting Associates, 2006

Heathfield, Susan, *Top Ten Ways to Retain Your Great Employees;* Heathfield Consulting Associates, 2006

Iyengar, Sheena; *The Art of Choosing*; 2011; Twelve Publishing

James, William; *The Principles of Psychology*; 1890, 1950; Dover Publications

Jansen, Julie; *I Don't Know What I Want, But I Know It's Not This;* Penguin Books, 2003

Kahneman, Daniel; *Thinking, Fast and Slow*; 2011; Farrar, Straus and Giroux

Kidder, Rushworth*; How Good People Make Tough Choices;* Quill, 2003

Kritzell and Logan*; Reinventing Your Career;* McGraw-Hill, 1997

Koch, Richard; *The 80/20 Principle*; 1998; Currency

Lore, Nicholas; *The Pathfinder;* Fireside, 1998

Martin, Judith; *Miss Manner's Guide for the Turn-of-*

the-Millenium; Fireside, 1990

McCormack, Mark; *What They Don't Teach You at Harvard Business School;* Bantam Press, 1988

McKay, Dawn Rosenberg, *How to Get Fired;* Careerplanning.com, 2006

McKay, Dawn Rosenberg, *Toward a More Civil Workplace;* Careerplanning.com, 2006

Paul, Margaret, PhD, *Do I Have To Give Up Me To Be Loved By You?;* Harper Collins, 1989

Pink, Daniel, *Free Agent Nation*; Warner Business Books, 2001

Pink, Daniel H.; *Drive*; 2009; Riverhead Books

Stanley, Thomas J. & Danko, William D.; *The Millionaire Next Door*; 1996; Pocket Books

Tieger and Barron-Tieger; *Do What You Are*; Little, Brown, 2001

Tracy, Brian, *Goals-How to Get Everything You Want;* Berrett-Koehler, 2003

WEB SITES
authentichappiness.org
homebusinessmag.com
humanmetrics.com
Kolbe.com
monster.ca
myersbriggs.org
psychologytoday.com

6,000,000 MINUTES ON THE CLOCK

psych.rochester.edu/SDT
stickK.com
teamtechnology.co.uk

6,000,000 MINUTES ON THE CLOCK

www.ingramcontent.com/pod-product-compliance
Lightning Source LLC
Chambersburg PA
CBHW070606300426
44113CB00010B/1428